AUTHOR

Peter Chandler

Peter Chandler is an independent employment law and health and safety consultant, and a Fellow of the Chartered Institute of Personnel and Development (CIPD). He is the author of several books in these and related fields and contributes to a number of Croner's loose-leaf publications, pocket guides and briefings. He has lectured widely on employment law and industrial relations issues and was engaged for four years as a freelance consultant on Croner's Employment Law Line.

INTRODUCTION

This glossary of terms forms part of your subscription to Croner's *Reference Book for Employers*. It provides definitions of commonly-used employment law and HR terms, with references to relevant legislation and cross-references to related items. A list of abbreviations is provided on page 2 for references to Acts and Regulations used throughout the book.

GLOSSARY OF EMPLOYMENT TERMS

LIST OF ABBREVIATIONS

Data Protection Act (DPA)
Disability Discrimination Act (DDA)
Employment Act (EA)
Employment Relations Act (ERA)
Equal Pay Act (EqPA)
Employment Tribunals Act (ETA)
Fixed-term Employees (Prevention of Less Favourable Treatment) Regulations (FTER)
Health and Safety at Work Act (HASAWA)
Human Rights Act (HRA)
Management of Health and Safety at Work Regulations (MHSAWR)
Maternity and Parental Leave, etc Regulations (MPLR)
National Minimum Wage Regulations (NMWR)
National Minimum Wages Act (NMWA)
Part-time Workers (Prevention of Less Favourable Treatment) Regulations (PTWR)
Race Relations Act (RRA)
Reporting of Injuries, Diseases and Dangerous Occurrences Regulations (RIDDOR)
Sex Discrimination Act (SDA)
Trade Union and Labour Relations (Consolidation) Act (TULRA)
Transfer of Undertakings (Protection of Employment) Regulations (TUPE)
Working Time Regulations (WTR)

A

ACAS　　　　　　See *Advisory, Conciliation and Arbitration Service*.

ACAS Arbitration Scheme　　　Introduced pursuant to s.212A of the **Trade Union and Labour Relations (Consolidation) Act 1992**, the ACAS Arbitration Scheme provides a voluntary alternative to employment tribunals for the resolution, by an ACAS-appointed independent arbitrator, of unfair dismissal disputes. The aim of the Scheme (which is available in England and Wales only) is to promote the settlement of such disputes in a confidential, informal, relatively fast and cost-efficient way. Unlike the handling of unfair dismissal complaints before the employment tribunals, the Scheme avoids the use of formal pleadings, and formal witness and documentary procedures. Strict rules of evidence do not apply and, as far as possible, instead of applying strict law or legal precedent, the arbitrator must take into account the general principles of fairness and good conduct, including, for example, the guidance in the ACAS Code of Practice on *Disciplinary and Grievance Procedures* or in its *Discipline at Work* handbook. Arbitral decisions and awards under the Scheme are final, with limited opportunities to appeal against or challenge the arbitrator's findings. Further details of the scheme may be obtained by telephoning ACAS Reader Limited on 0870 2422090 or by accessing the ACAS website at *www.acas.org.uk/arbitration.htm*. (*Sources:* TULRA 1992, s.212A; **ACAS Arbitration Scheme (England and Wales) Order 2001.**)

accident book　　　Under the **Social Security (Claims and Payments) Regulations 1979** (as amended), every employee who sustains an injury at work, however minor, should report the incident to his or her immediate supervisor without delay and enter the relevant particulars (or see to it that those particulars are recorded on his or her behalf) in an accident book maintained by his or her employer for that very purpose. In organisations with fewer that 10 people on the payroll, a simple exercise book will suffice. Larger organisations should use the prescribed form of Accident Book — Form BI 510 (ISBN 0117019860) — copies of which may be purchased from The Stationery Office. Every entry in the accident book must be maintained for at least three years from the date on which that entry was made. See also *accident investigation*.

accident investigation

Employers have a duty under the **Social Security (Claims and Payments) Regulations 1979** (as amended) to investigate the circumstances of every workplace injury reported to them and recorded in the accident book. If there is any discrepancy between the outcome of the investigations and the injured employee's version of events, the safety officer or investigating manager or supervisor must make a note of that discrepancy alongside the relevant entry in the accident book and (advisedly) on the employee's personal file.

accident reporting

Under the **Reporting of Injuries, Diseases and Dangerous Occurrences Regulations 1995** (RIDDOR), every employer is duty-bound to inform the relevant enforcing authority immediately (eg by telephone or e-mail) of any workplace accident that results in the death of, or major injury to any person (whether employee or a member of the general public). A follow-up report (using form F2508) must be sent to the enforcing authority within the next 10 days. See also *accident book* and *accident investigation*.

accompanied, right to be

A worker who is required or invited by his or her employer to attend a disciplinary or grievance hearing has the legal right to be accompanied at the hearing by a single companion who may be another of the employer's workers, a shop steward or a full-time trade union official. The chosen companion must be permitted to address the hearing (but not to answer questions on the worker's behalf) and must be paid his or her normal wages or salary while present at the hearing. If the chosen companion is unable to attend at the time proposed for the hearing, the employer must postpone the hearing to a time proposed by the worker falling within the period of five working days immediately following the day originally proposed by the employer. (*Source:* ERA 1999, s.10.)

action short of dismissal

Employees and other workers have the legal right not to be victimised or subjected to any other detriment (short of dismissal) for exercising or presuming to exercise their statutory employment rights for questioning or challenging any infringement of those rights, or for taking action to enforce those rights before an employment tribunal. The amount of compensation that may be awarded by employment tribunals in such cases is substantial. The relevant legislation is to be found in the **Trade Union and Labour Relations (Consolidation) Act 1992**, the **Employment Rights Act 1996**, the **Sex Discrimination Act 1975**, the **Race Relations Act 1976**, and the **Disability Discrimination Act 1995**.

additional award of compensation

If an employment tribunal upholds an employee's complaint of unfair dismissal, it may make an order requiring the employer to reinstate or re-engage that employee. However, before doing so, the tribunal must first consider the wishes of the employee, the extent to which he or she contributed to the dismissal (if at all), and whether or not it would be practicable for the employer to comply with any such order (disregarding the fact that the employer may already have engaged a permanent replacement). An employer who refuses to comply (or to comply fully) with a tribunal order for the reinstatement or re-engagement of an unfairly dismissed employee, will be ordered by the tribunal to pay the employee an additional amount of compensation (of between 26 and 52 weeks' pay) — that is to say, compensation in addition to any basic or compensatory award of compensation for unfair dismissal payable to that same employee. (*Source:* ERA 1996, ss.112–117.) See also *basic award of compensation*, *compensatory award* and *supplementary award*.

additional maternity leave
On completion of her ordinary maternity leave period, a pregnant employee with one or more year's continuous service at the beginning of the 11th week before her expected week of childbirth (EWC) (and whose EWC begins before 6 April 2003) is entitled to an additional period of maternity leave that continues until the end of the period of 29 weeks that begins on the Sunday of the week in which childbirth occurred. (*Sources:* ERA 1996, s.73; MPLR 1999.)

A pregnant employee whose EWC begins on or after 6 April 2003, and who has completed a minimum of 26 weeks' continuous service by the end of the 15th week before her EWC, is entitled to take up to 26 weeks' additional maternity leave beginning on the day immediately following the day on which her ordinary maternity leave period ends. (*Sources:* ERA 1996, s.73; and the **Maternity and Parental Leave Regulations 1999**, as amended by the **Maternity and Parental Leave (Amendment) Regulations 2002**.)

adolescent worker A worker under the age of 18 who has lawfully left school. See also *hours of work: workers under the age of 18, risk assessment* and *young worker*.

adoption agency To qualify for adoption leave, an employee must (amongst other things) have been newly-matched with a child for adoption by an approved "adoption agency" as defined by s.1(4) of the **Adoption Act 1976** and (in relation to Scotland) by s.1(4) of the **Adoption (Scotland) Act 1978**. It follows that adoption leave and pay is not available in circumstances where a child is not newly-matched for adoption, eg when a step-parent adopts his or her partner's children. (*Source:* **Paternity and Adoption Leave Regulations 2002**, regulation 2.)

adoption leave An adoptive parent has the right under the **Paternity and Adoption Leave Regulations 2002** to take up to 26 weeks' ordinary adoption leave followed immediately (subject to certain conditions) by up to 26 weeks' additional adoption leave. To be eligible for adoption leave, an employee must have been newly-matched with a child for adoption by an approved adoption agency, and have been continuously employed by his or her employer for 26 or more weeks by the end of the week in which he or she was formally notified of being matched with a child for adoption. The right to adoption leave is available to one only of a couple (male or female) who have adopted a child. It is for them to decide which of them takes adoption leave. The other partner (if employed) may qualify for paternity leave (adoption). (*Sources:* ERA 1996, ss.75A and 75B; **Paternity and Adoption Leave Regulations 2002**.) See also *statutory adoption pay*.

adoption pay period The period of 26 weeks beginning with the day immediately following the day on which an employee begins his or her ordinary adoption leave. See *statutory adoption pay*.

adult worker

A worker who has attained the age of 18.

advertisements, discriminatory

An employer (employment agency or business) who (or which) publishes, or causes to be published, any advertisement which indicates, or might reasonably be understood as indicating, an intention to discriminate against any job applicant — on grounds of sex or race — is guilty of an offence and liable, on summary conviction, to a fine of up to £5000. Use of a job description with a sexual connotation (such as waiter, salesgirl, postman or stewardess) will be taken to indicate an intention to discriminate, unless the advertisement contains an indication to the contrary.

The publisher of an unlawful advertisement will not be guilty of an offence if he or she proves that the advertisement was published in reliance on a statement made to him or her by the person who caused it to be published to the effect that the publication would not be unlawful and that it was reasonable for him or her to rely on that statement. Similar provisions relating to discriminatory advertisements (not liable to criminal prosecution) are to be found in the **Trade Union and Labour Relations (Consolidation) Act 1992** (discrimination on grounds of trade union membership or non-membership) and in the **Disability Discrimination Act 1995**. (*Sources*: SDA 1975, s.38; RRA 1976, s.29; TULRA 1992, s.137; DDA 1995, s.11.)

Advisory, Conciliation and Arbitration Service

Originally established under the **Employment Protection Act 1975**, the Advisory, Conciliation and Arbitration Service (or ACAS, as it is more commonly known) continues in existence under the **Trade Union and Labour Relations (Consolidation) Act 1992**. ACAS is a body corporate, independent of Government control, whose general duty it is to promote the improvement of industrial relations. ACAS may issue codes of practice; offer to advise, conciliate or arbitrate where a trade dispute exists or is apprehended; designate some of its officers to perform the functions of conciliation officers under any enactment relating to matters that are (or could be) the subject of proceedings before an employment tribunal; and, in cases of alleged unfair dismissal (and with the agreement of both parties) refer the dispute for determination by an ACAS-appointed independent arbitrator under the ACAS Arbitration Scheme. (*Sources:* TULRA, Part IV, Chapters III and IV; **ACAS Arbitration Scheme (England and Wales) Order 2001.**)

age discrimination Discrimination on grounds of age is not yet illegal in the UK. However, with the publication on 2 December 2000 of Council Directive 2000/78/EC "establishing a general framework for equal treatment in employment and occupation", the UK and other EU Member States have until 2 December 2003 in which to introduce domestic legislation outlawing discrimination in employment on grounds of age, religion or belief, disability or sexual orientation. Article 18 of the Directive nonetheless allows that, in order to take account of particular conditions, Member States may, if necessary, have an additional period of three years, from 2 December 2003, to implement the Directive's provisions on age and disability discrimination. It is not yet clear whether the UK Government intends to take advantage of that permitted extension.

agency worker A worker (other than a self-employed person) supplied by a person ("the agent") to do work for another ("the principal") under a contract of employment or any other contract (whether express or implied) made between the agent and the principal. Agency workers (or agency "temps") enjoy the protection afforded to all workers by Part II of the **Employment Rights Act 1996 (Protection of Wages)**; the **National Minimum Wage Act 1998** (s.34); and the **Working Time Regulations 1998**; and have the right not to be discriminated against on grounds of sex, race, disability or trade union membership or non-membership. They have the right also under s.47B of the 1996 Act not to be subjected to any detriment (including termination of their contracts) by any act, or any deliberate failure to act, by their employers done on the grounds that they have made a protected disclosure. See also *worker*.

annual holidays

Every worker (part-time, full-time, temporary, seasonal or casual) has the legal right to a minimum of four weeks' paid holiday in every holiday year; in short, a right to be physically absent from the workplace for a total of four weeks and to be paid a normal week's pay in respect of each of those weeks. Workers must take their four weeks' holiday in the holiday year in which they fall due (the holiday year being the period of 12 months that begins on the day the worker starts work and on each subsequent anniversary of that day; or which is the agreed holiday year for the organisation in question). Unused days of holiday may not be carried forward into the next holiday year; nor is a worker entitled to be paid money in lieu of those unused days. Bank and public holidays may be included in those four weeks unless (as is likely) there is a term to the contrary in the worker's contract or the workers in question are traditionally entitled to bank and public holidays in addition to their annual holidays. A worker who resigns or is dismissed part-way through a holiday year is entitled to accrued holiday pay on the termination of his or her employment (less a deduction in respect of holidays already taken), even if employed for just one or two days when his or her employment comes to an end. Holidays to which an employee or other worker is contractually entitled may be offset against the statutory entitlement, and vice versa. (*Source:* **Working Time Regulations 1998**, as amended (regulations 13 to 17.)

annualised hours

Under a so-called "annualised hours" contract, an employee agrees to work a specified number of hours over a particular period, usually 12 months, based on a notional working week of, say, 35 hours. The employee would receive the same weekly wage or salary, week in and week out (regardless of the number of hours he or she actually works in any one week). If, for example, the notional working week is one of 35 hours (7 hours per day), the total number of hours to be worked by such an employee over a 52-week period would be 1820 hours, reduced to 1624 hours to take account of bank and public holidays and paid annual holidays (ie 28 x 7). Employees on annualised hours contracts would normally be expected to forewarn their employers, at least one month beforehand, of the number of hours they intend to work in the following month. Employers, for their part, would reserve the right to require such an employee to attend for work on a particular day in order to deal with problems associated with unexpected absenteeism or a surge in business activity. Employees on annualised contracts would not be paid overtime until they had completed the agreed number of working hours in a particular 12-month period.

antenatal care

Every pregnant employee, regardless of her length of service at the material time, has the legal right to be permitted a reasonable amount of paid time off work for the purpose of receiving antenatal care, as advised by her doctor, registered midwife or registered health visitor. If asked to do so, on the second (but not the first) occasion that she seeks permission to take time off for this purpose, she must produce for her employer's inspection a certificate signed by her doctor, midwife or health visitor stating that she is pregnant, as well as an appointment card or some other document confirming that she has made one or more appointments to attend at an antenatal clinic. (*Source:* ERA 1996 ss.55–57.)

appropriate representatives

When planning collective redundancies or a TUPE transfer, employers are duty bound to consult (ie discuss their proposals with) the appropriate representatives. These are either trade union-appointed representatives or (if there is no trade union representation) representatives elected by the affected employees to represent their interests in discussions with their employer. (*Sources:* TULRA 1992, ss.188–192; **TUPE Regulations 1981**, regulations 10–11A).

associated employers

Any two employers are to be treated as associated if:

    (a) one is a company of which the other (directly or indirectly) has control, or

    (b) both are companies of which a third person (directly or indirectly) has control

(*Source:* ERA 1996, s.231.)

Asylum and Immigration Act 1996

Any UK employer who employs a foreign national aged 16 or over, who is either an illegal immigrant or does not have the legal and subsisting right to take up employment in the UK, is liable to prosecution under the **Asylum and Immigration Act 1996**. The penalty on summary conviction is a fine of up to £5000 for each and every offence. Prosecutions may be brought not only against the offending business or company but also against any director, company secretary, personnel officer, manager or supervisor who is directly responsibly for a breach of the 1996 Act. See also *work permits*.

automatically unfair dismissal

It is inadmissible and automatically unfair to dismiss any employee (or to select such an employee for redundancy) on grounds of sex, marital status, gender reassignment, race, colour, nationality, national or ethnic origins, disability, or trade union membership (or non-membership). It is, likewise, unlawful to dismiss an employee for asserting his or her statutory employment rights, or for questioning or challenging any alleged infringement of those rights (whether before an employment tribunal or otherwise) or for having made a protected disclosure. A complaint of unlawful dismissal (or unlawful selection for redundancy) on such grounds may be presented to an employment tribunal regardless of the employee's age or length of service at the material time.

B

bank and public holidays

In the absence of any express or implied contractual term to the contrary, employees and other workers have no statutory or common law right to time off work (paid or unpaid) on a bank or public holiday. **Under the Working Time Regulations 1998** (as amended), an employer may incorporate bank and public holidays in the four weeks' paid annual holidays to which workers are entitled under those Regulations, unless, as is more often the case, those workers have the express or implied contractual right to take bank and public holidays in addition to those annual holidays. To that end, the written statement of employment particulars necessarily issued to all employees must include particulars of any terms and conditions relating to holidays, including public holidays and holiday pay (the particulars given being sufficient to enable the employee's entitlement, including any entitlement to accrued holiday pay on the termination of employment, to be precisely calculated). (*Sources:* **Banking and Financial Dealings Act 1971**; ERA 1996, s.1.)

basic award of compensation

There are three elements to an award of compensation for unfair dismissal. These are: the basic award, the compensatory award and the additional award. In prescribed circumstances, a supplementary award may also be awarded. The basic award is calculated by reference to an employee's age and length of service at the time of his or her dismissal, by much the same method as that used to calculate a statutory redundancy payment (except that years of continuous service before the age of 18 are also included in calculations). The basic award may be reduced by such amount as an employment tribunal considers appropriate if the evidence reveals (a) that the dismissed employee unreasonably refused an offer by his or her employer to reinstate him in his employment in all respects as if he or she had not been dismissed and/or (b) that, the employee's conduct before his or her dismissal contributed to a greater or lesser extent to his or her own dismissal. It may also be reduced (or further reduced) by the amount of any redundancy payment previously awarded by the tribunal in respect of the same dismissal or any payment made the employer to the employee by way of a redundancy or severance payment (statutory or otherwise).

An employee held by an employment tribunal to have been unfairly dismissed or selected for redundancy for performing (or proposing to perform) his or her functions as a designated, trade union-appointed or employee-elected safety representative; or as a workforce representative; a pension scheme trustee; or as a trade union or employee-elected employee representative (or candidate for election), will be awarded a minimum basic award of £3500. The basic award of compensation for unfair dismissal will be the equivalent of two weeks' pay if (in a redundancy situation), the employee had not unreasonably refused an offer of suitable alternative work or would not otherwise have qualified for a statutory redundancy payment. (*Source:* ERA 1996 ss.119–122.) See also *redundancy payment*.

Basic Disclosure   See *Criminal Records Bureau*.

betting work   Work at a racing track in England or Wales for a bookmaker which consists of dealing with betting transactions and work in a licensed betting office. The term "betting transactions" includes the collection or payment of winnings on a bet and any transaction in which one or more of the parties is acting as a bookmaker. (*Source:* ERA 1996, s.233.)

betting worker   An employee who, under his contract of employment, is or may be required to do betting work. (*Source:* ERA 1996, s.233.) See *Sunday working*.

blue pencil test   See *restrictive covenant*.

breach of contract   There is a breach of contract if a party to that contract fails to discharge one or more of his or her obligations under that contract. In the case of a contract of employment, a breach by the employer of a fundamental term of that contract (once accepted) will ordinarily entitle the injured party (the employee) to resign and pursue a complaint of unfair constructive dismissal and/or an action for damages before a civil court or employment tribunal. A breach (or repudiation) of a fundamental term of contract by an employee (once accepted by the employer) entitles the employer to bring the contract to an end. See also *gross misconduct* and *summary dismissal*.

Since 12 July 1994, the employment tribunals have had jurisdiction to entertain wrongful dismissal and other breach of contract claims that arise, or remain unresolved, on the termination of an employee's contract of employment. However, there is an upper limit of £25,000 on the amount of damages that can be awarded by the tribunals in such cases. Claims for damages in excess of that amount remain the province of the ordinary courts, as do personal injury claims and claims relating to tied accommodation. The same applies to claims relating to intellectual property, obligations of confidence, and restrictive covenants. (*Sources:* **Employment Tribunals Extension of Jurisdiction (England and Wales) Order 1994**; and the **Employment Tribunals Extension of Jurisdiction (Scotland) Order 1994**).

breastfeeding mothers

See *new or expectant mothers*.

burden of proof (or onus probandi)

The duty of proving one's case. In an unfair dismissal case, it is for the respondent employer to show the reason (or, if more than one, the principal reason) for the dismissal, and that it is one of four permitted reasons for dismissal or some other substantial reason of a kind such as to justify the dismissal of an employee holding the position which the employee held. It is then for the tribunal to determine from the evidence before it whether the employer had acted reasonably or unreasonably in treating that reason as a sufficient reason for dismissing the employee. In sex discrimination cases, once the complainant employee has adduced evidence sufficient to establish a *prima facie* case of unlawful discrimination, the burden of proof shifts to the respondent employer. In short, the employer must then persuade the employment tribunal that the employee had not been the victim of unlawful discrimination. (*Sources:* ERA 1996, s.98; **Sex Discrimination Act 1975**, s.63A, inserted by the **Sex Discrimination (Indirect Discrimination and Burden of Proof) Regulations 2001**.)

business

This term includes a trade or profession and includes any activity carried on by a body of persons (whether corporate or unincorporated). (*Source:* ERA 1996, s.235.)

C

capability

One of the five permitted reasons for dismissal. In relation to an employee, "capability" means his or her capability assessed by reference to skill, aptitude, health or any other physical or mental quality. (*Source:* ERA 1996, s.98(3).)

care, duty of

An employer has a common law and implied contractual duty to take reasonable care for the health and safety at work of each and every employee. An employee or other worker who is injured in the course of his or her employment as a direct consequence of his or her employer's negligent failure to comply with that duty, may pursue a claim for damages in the ordinary courts. Against that possibility, every employer is duty-bound to insure (and maintain insurance) "against liability for bodily injury or disease sustained by his employees and arising out of and in the course of their employment".

The insurance cover (for a minimum of £5 million) must be effected with an authorised insurer. The Certificate of Employer's Liability Insurance must be kept available for inspection by the relevant enforcing authority (ie a Health and Safety Executive (HSE) or local authority inspectors) while a copy (or copies) of that Certificate must be displayed in the employer's premises in a position (or positions) where it can be easily seen and read by every employee. A failure to comply with these requirements is a criminal offence for which the penalty on summary conviction is a fine of up to £2500 (and a further fine of £2500 a day for each day of continued non-compliance). (*Source:* **Employers' Liability (Compulsory Insurance) Act 1969.**)

cash shortages

A deficit arising in relation to amounts received in connection with retail transactions. Deductions from the wages of a worker in retail employment (or demands for payment from such a worker) on account of cash shortages (or stock deficiencies) are permissible if, but only if, there is an express term in that worker's contract (signed at the time his or her employment began) authorising such deductions; or if the worker has previously agreed (in writing) to any such deduction or payment and the circumstances in which such deductions or payments may be made. Furthermore, the maximum amount that may be deducted from a worker's wages (and the maximum of any demand for payment) in respect of one or more cash shortages may not exceed one-tenth of the gross amount of the wages payable to the worker on that day.

However, that restriction does not apply to a deduction made from the final instalment of wages payable to a worker on the termination of his or her employment (or any demand for payment at that time) in respect of cash shortages (or stock deficiencies). A complaint that an employer has made one or more unlawful deductions from a worker's wages, or had demanded and received one or more unlawful payments, may be referred to an employment tribunal. If such a complaint is upheld, the employer will be ordered to make restitution. (*Source:* ERA 1996, Part II.)

Central Arbitration Committee

The Central Arbitration Committee (CAC) is the senior standing arbitration tribunal in Great Britain. The CAC comprises a chairman and one or more deputy chairman appointed by the Secretary of State (after consultation with ACAS and other persons) and members with experience both as representatives of employers and representatives of employees. Members normally hold office for a maximum of five years. Cases brought before the CAC are normally heard by the chairman (or a deputy chairman) and two other members. The CAC is empowered to arbitrate to resolve a trade dispute (if asked to do so by both parties to the dispute) and deals with complaints by a recognised independent trade union concerning an employer's alleged failure to disclose information required to be disclosed under s.183 of the **Trade Union and Labour Relations (Consolidation) Act 1992** for the purposes of collective bargaining. The CAC also has a significant part to play in relation to an independent trade union's request for recognition by an employer for collective bargaining purposes. (*Source:* TULRA 1992, ss.70A, 70B, 181, 183, 259-265, and Schedule A1.)

certificate of expected confinement

A certificate (Form Mat B1) or alternative document, signed by a woman's doctor or registered midwife, stating her expected week of childbirth. When notifying her employer of the date on which she intends to begin her ordinary maternity leave, a pregnant employee must produce Form Mat B1 or its equivalent for her employer's inspection (but only if ask to do so). If, on the other hand, a pregnant employee qualifies for statutory maternity pay (SMP), her employer must be supplied with the certificate (a copy of which should be kept on file) before SMP payments can begin. (*Sources:* **Maternity and Parental Leave Regulations 1999**, regulation 4(b); **Statutory Maternity Pay Regulations 1986**, regulation 22; **Statutory Maternity Pay (Medical Evidence) Regulations 1987**.)

Certification Officer   An independent statutory officer appointed by the Secretary of State for Trade and Industry (after consultation with the Advisory, Conciliation and Arbitration Service), whose primary role it is to maintain a list of trade unions, to issue certificates of independence and to ensure that trade unions on the list comply with statutory requirements concerning their membership and accounting records.

For these purposes, the Certification Officer and his staff of inspectors may investigate a trade union's financial affairs, scrutinise their annual returns and the management of their political and superannuation funds; determine whether unions meet (or continue to meet) the statutory test of independence; take steps to ensure that trade unions comply with their statutory duties in relation to the election of senior union officials; deal with complaints by union members concerning alleged breaches of trade union legislation or trade union rules (including alleged breaches by unions of their statutory duties to elect senior officers); and make enforcement orders to remedy failures to comply with the law. The Certification Officer is also empowered to hear complaints by union members relating to the misuse of union funds for political purposes — where the union does not have a political fund — and complaints about a union's alleged failure to comply with the rules relating to political fund ballots. Certain decisions of the Certification Officer may be appealed on a point of law to the Employment Appeal Tribunal. (*Source:* TULRA 1992, Part I.)

change of employer The continuity of an employee's period of employment is not broken where:

- a trade, business or undertaking is transferred from one person to another
- an employer dies and the employee is taken into the employment of the employer's personal representative or trustees
- there is a change in the partners, personal representatives or trustees that employ a person
- an employee is taken into the employment of an associated employee.

(*Source:* ERA 1996, s.218.)

"check-off" system (union dues) An employer must not deduct trade union dues (ie membership subscriptions) from any worker's pay packet (whether or not in accordance with "check-off" arrangements previously agreed with the relevant trade union) without the worker's prior written consent. If the worker subsequently writes asking the employer to stop deducting union dues from his or her wages or salary, the employer must act on that request on the next available pay day. A worker may complain to an employment tribunal that his employer has deducted union dues from his pay in contravention of these requirements. The complaint must be presented within the period of three months beginning with the date on which the unauthorised deduction was made or (if there have been a number of such deductions) the date on which the last of those deductions was made. If the complaint is upheld, the tribunal will make a declaration to that effect and will order the employer to make restitution.

The itemised pay statement issued to every employee in accordance with s.8 of the **Employment Rights Act 1996** must contain (amongst other things) particulars of any fixed deduction (including a deduction in respect of trade union dues) from the gross amount of the wages or salary payable to that employee. (*Source:* TULRA 1992, s.68.)

child-bearing age, women of

Regulation 3 of the **Management of Health and Safety at Work Regulations 1999** imposes a duty on all employers (large as well as small) to carry out a risk assessment designed to identify workplace hazards and their associated risks, and to take appropriate steps to eliminate or minimise those risks. The Regulations further state that "where the persons working in an undertaking include women of child-bearing age, and the work is of a kind that could involve risk, by reason of her condition, to the health and safety of a new or expectant mother, or to that of her baby, from any processes or working conditions, or physical, biological or chemical agents (including those specified in Annexes I and II of Council Directive 92/85/EEC), the risk assessment exercise must include an assessment of that risk. If there is nothing that can be done to avoid that risk, the employer must either alter the woman's working conditions or hours of work or, if that proves unsuccessful, suspend her from work for so long as is necessary to avoid that risk". (*Source*: MHSAWR, regulation 16.) See also *suspension on maternity grounds*.

childbirth

Means the birth of a living child or the birth of a child, whether living or dead, after 24 weeks of pregnancy. (*Source:* ERA 1996, s.235.)

**children,
employment of**

In law, a child is a person who is not over compulsory school age. Legislation prohibiting or restricting the employment of children under the age of 16 is to be found in the **Employment of Women, Young Persons and Children Act 1920** (as amended), the **Children and Young Persons Act 1993** (as amended), the **Education (Work Experience) Act 1973**, the **Education Act 1993**, and in local authority bye-laws. School age children may not be employed in any industrial undertaking. Furthermore, no school age child may be employed:

- if under the age of 14
- before the close of school hours on any day
- before 7.00am or after 7.00pm on any day
- for more than two hours on a school day
- for more than two hours on a Sunday
- for more than eight hours (or, if under the age of 15, for more than five hours) on any day (other than a Sunday) which is not a school day
- for more than 12 hours in any week in which he or she is required to attend school
- for more than 35 hours (or, if under the age of 15, for more than 25 hours) in any week in which he or she is not required to attend school
- for more than four hours on any day without a rest break of at least one hour during that spell of employment
- at any time in a year unless, at that time, he or she has had, or could still have, at least two consecutive weeks without employment
- to do any work other than light work ("light work" being work of a kind that is unlikely to affect the safety, health or development of a school age child or to interfere with the child's education or regular and punctual attendance at school.

Employers seeking to employ school age children must apply to their nearest local education authority for an Employment

Certificate. The authority will provide an application form and a copy of its byelaws on the employment of children. The consent of the child's parents or guardians will also be required. The latter must also be notified of any risks associated with the work in question and the steps taken by the putative employer to eliminate or minimise those risks. See also *risk assessment*.

closed shop

A closed shop (or union membership agreement) is an understanding or agreement between an employer and one or more trade unions under which the employer agrees not to employ (or to continue to employ) any person who is not a member of one or other of the trade unions party to that agreement. Nowadays, the closed shop is a legal irrelevancy, and cannot be used to justify an employer's refusal to interview or employ a job applicant who is not a member of the trade union in question (or of any union). Indeed, closed shop or no, it is unlawful to refuse to employ a person because he or she is, or is not, a member of a trade union, or because he or she is unwilling to accept a requirement to take steps to become, or cease to be, or to remain or not to become, a member of a trade union, or to make payments or suffer deductions from his or her wages or salary in the event of his or her not being a member of a trade union. A person denied (or who suspects that he or she has been denied) employment on such grounds may complain to an employment tribunal and will be awarded substantial compensation (subject to a maximum of £53,500) if the complaint is upheld. (*Source:* TULRA 1992, ss.137 and 140.)

codes of practice

Bodies such as the Advisory, Conciliation and Arbitration Service (ACAS), the Equal Opportunities Commission, the Commission for Racial Equality, the Disability Rights Commission, the Health and Safety Commission and the Secretary of State for Trade and Industry, are empowered to issue codes of practice providing practical guidance for employers and employees on their duties and obligations under employment law and health and safety legislation. That right is also available to the Information Commissioner (formerly the Data Protection Commissioner) under the **Data Protection Act 1998**. A failure on the part of any person to observe any provision of an approved code of practice does not of itself render him or her liable to proceedings before a tribunal or court. However, in any such proceedings, any code of practice issued by one or other of the bodies mentioned above is admissible in evidence, and any provision of the code which appears to be relevant to any question arising in those proceedings shall be taken into account in determining that question. (*Sources* HASAWA 1974, s.17; SDA 1975, s.56A; RRA 1976, s.47; TULRA 1992, s.207; DDA 1995, s.53A.)

collective agreement Any agreement or arrangement made by a trade union and an employer or employers' association relating to one or more of the following:

(a) terms and conditions of employment, or the physical conditions in which workers are required to work

(b) engagement or non-engagement, or termination or suspension of employment or the duties of employment, of workers

(c) allocation of work between workers or groups of workers

(d) matters of discipline

(e) a worker's membership or non-membership of a trade union

(f) facilities for officials of trade unions; and

(g) machinery for negotiation or consultation, and other procedures, relating to any of the above matters, including the recognition by employers or employers' associations of the right of a trade union to represent workers in negotiation or consultation. (*Source:* TULRA 1992.)

The written statement of employment particulars prescribed by s.1 of the **Employment Rights Act 1996** must include particulars of "any collective agreements which directly affect the terms and conditions of the employment including, where the employer is not a party [to that agreement] the persons by whom, they were made".

collective redundancies

See *consultations: collective redundancies* and *redundancy payment*.

Commission for Racial Equality

Established under s.43 of the **Race Relations Act 1976**, the Commission for Racial Equality (CRE) comprises a minimum of eight (but no more than 15) commissioners, including a chairman and one or more deputy chairmen appointed by the Secretary of State on a full-time or part-time basis. The CRE's role is to work towards the elimination of racial discrimination, to promote equality of opportunity and good relations between different racial groups, and to monitor compliance with the 1976 Act. It is empowered to issue codes of practice, conduct investigations, serve non-discrimination notices, provide help and advice to persons pursuing complaints of unlawful discrimination, and apply to the courts for injunctions or orders designed to restrain the activities of persistent offenders. (*Source:* RRA 1976, Part VII.)

comparable full-time worker

For the purposes of the **Part-time Workers (Prevention of Less Favourable Treatment) Regulations 2000**, a worker is a full-time worker if he or she is paid wholly or in part by reference to the time he or she works and, having regard to the custom and practice in the undertaking in which he or she is employed, is identifiable as a full-time worker. A full-time worker is a "comparable full-time worker" in relation to a part-time worker if both workers are employed under the same type of contract and engaged in the same or broadly similar work (having regard, where relevant, to whether they have a similar level of qualifications, skills and experience); and the full-time worker is based at the same establishment as the part-time worker or, where there is no full-time worker working or based at that establishment who satisfies the above requirements, works or is based at a different establishment and satisfies those requirements. (*Source:* PTWR 2000, regulation 2.) See also *less favourable treatment* and *part-time worker*.

comparable permanent employee

A term used in the context of an employee's statutory rights under the **Fixed-term Employees (Prevention of Less Favourable Treatment) Regulations 2002**. For the purposes of those Regulations, an employee is a "comparable permanent employee" in relation to a fixed-term employee if, at the time when the treatment that is alleged to be less favourable to the fixed-term employee takes place, both employees are employed by the same employer and engaged in the same or broadly similar work, having regard where relevant to whether they have a similar level of qualifications and skills; and the permanent employee works or is based at the same establishment as the fixed-term employee or, where there is no comparable permanent employee working or based at that establishment who satisfies those requirements, works or is based at a different establishment and satisfies those requirements. For the above purposes, an employee is not a comparable permanent employee if his or her employment has ceased (FTER, regulation 2).

compensatory award

There are three elements to an award of compensation for unfair dismissal. These are: the basic award, the compensatory award and the additional award. In prescribed circumstances, a supplementary award may also be awarded. The compensatory award is such an amount as an employment tribunal considers just and equitable in all the circumstances, having regard to the loss sustained by an employee in consequence of his or her dismissal, in so far as that loss is attributable to the action taken by the employee's employer, and includes any expenses reasonably incurred by the employee in consequence of the dismissal; loss of any benefit that the employee might reasonably have expected to have had but for his or her dismissal; and the loss of any entitlement (or potential entitlement) to a redundancy payment in excess of that included in the basic award of compensation ordered to be paid to the employee. In determining the amount of any compensatory award, the tribunal will apply the same rule concerning the duty of a person to mitigate his or her loss (eg efforts to find suitable alternative employment) as applies to damages recoverable under the common law of England and Wales or Scotland. If an employment tribunal finds that an unfairly dismissed employee contributed to any extent to his or her own dismissal, it will reduce the amount of the compensatory award by such proportion as it considers just and equitable having regard to that finding. (*Source:* ERA 1996, ss.123 and 124.)

The current (2003/04) upper limit on the amount of the compensatory award is £53,500. That figure is reviewed each year in line with rises or falls in the September on September Retail Prices Index. (*Source:* ERA 1999, s.34.) That upper limit may be exceeded to the extent necessary to fully reflect the losses sustained by an employee when an order for his or her reinstatement or re-engagement is made or not fully complied with. Furthermore, there is no upper limit on the amount of any compensatory award that may be awarded to an employee (or other worker) held to have been unfairly dismissed (or unfairly selected for redundancy) in health and safety cases or for having made a protected disclosure. (*Source:* ERA 1996, s.124(1A).)

complaints to employment tribunals

Complaints to the employment tribunals concerning a breach (or an alleged breach) of an employee or other worker's contractual or statutory rights must normally be presented to the nearest regional office of the Employment Tribunals Service within three months of the date on which that breach or failure occurred, or within such further period as the tribunal considers reasonable in a case where it is satisfied that it was not reasonably practicable for the complaint to be presented before the end of that period of three months. Complaints should be lodged on Form IT1 (Originating Application to an Employment Tribunal). (*Source:* ERA 1996, various.)

compromise agreement

A form of legally-binding agreement for the resolution of any workplace dispute that could lead to (or has prompted the commencement of) proceedings before an employment tribunal (eg a dispute relating to an alleged infringement of an employee's statutory rights, including his or her right not to be unfairly dismissed). An employee who has concluded a valid and binding compromise agreement with his or her employer is thereby precluded from bringing (or continuing with proceedings) before an employment tribunal. To be valid, the agreement must be in writing, must relate to the particular proceedings; and must be signed by both parties.

Before signing the agreement, the employee must first have obtained advice from a relevant independent advisor as to the term and effect of the proposed agreement (in particular, its effect on the employee's ability to pursue his or her rights before an employment tribunal). Furthermore, the advisor must be insured or otherwise indemnified against any subsequent claim for damages arising out of his or her failure to give the correct advice. Finally, the agreement must identify the advisor by name and state that the conditions regulating compromise agreements have been satisfied. (*Source:* ERA 1996, s.203.)

Similar provisions concerning compromise agreements are to be found in the **Sex Discrimination Act 1975**, the **Race Relations Act 1976**, the **Trade Union and Labour Relations (Consolidation) Act 1992**, the **Disability Discrimination Act 1995**, the **Working Time Regulations 1998** (as amended), the **National Minimum Wage Act 1998**, the **Part-time Workers (Prevention of Less Favourable Treatment) Regulations 2000**, and in the **Fixed-term Employees (Prevention of Less Favourable Treatment) Regulations 2002**. See also *COT 3 agreement* and *ACAS Arbitration Scheme*.

compulsory maternity leave

An employee planning to return to work before the end of her ordinary maternity leave period may not lawfully do so during the so-called "compulsory maternity leave" period, that is to say, within two weeks of giving birth (or within four weeks of that date if she works in a factory). That same restriction applies to job applicants who have recently given birth. An employer who contravenes these prohibitions is guilty of an offence and liable, on summary conviction, to a fine of up to £500. (*Sources:* ERA 1996, s.72; **Public Health Act 1936**, s.205.)

compulsory school age   The period during which a child must remain at school. In England and Wales the school leaving date for a child who turns 16 on or after the beginning of a school year is the last Friday in June. A child who turns 16 after that last Friday in June, but before the beginning of the next school year, may likewise lawfully leave school on that same last Friday in June. In Scotland, a child who turns 16 during the period from 1 March to 30 September, inclusive, may leave school on 31 May of that same year. Children whose 16th birthdays occur outside that period must remain at school until the first day of the Christmas holidays. (*Sources:* **Education Act 1996**, s.8; **Education (Scotland) Act 1980**, s.31; **Education (School Leaving Date) Order 1997.**)

computerised records   An employer (the data controller) who holds personal data about an employee or other worker (the data subject) on computer or in some other computerised format (eg a floppy disc) must be prepared to reveal to the worker in question the nature of that data, why it is being held, how it is being used and to whom it is, has been, or is likely to be disclosed. Furthermore, on payment of a fee of up to £10, the worker has the right to be supplied with hard copies of that data (in an intelligible form) within 40 days of submitting a written request for access to that data. Furthermore, if a computer is used (or programmed) to evaluate or make decisions about an employee or other worker's performance, competence, reliability, conduct, suitability for promotion, etc the worker has the right also to be informed of the logic involved in that process and, where appropriate, to write asking for an assurance that no decision affecting him or her is taken solely on that basis. For further details, see *data protection*. (*Source:* DPA 1998, Part II.)

31

conciliation officer   An officer designated as such by the Advisory, Conciliation and Arbitration Service (ACAS). As the title suggests, the role of a conciliation officer is to conciliate in matters that are (or could be) the subject of proceedings before an employment tribunal. Where an application has been made to an employment tribunal, and a copy of it has been sent to a conciliation officer, it is the latter's duty to intervene with a view to promoting a settlement of the proceedings without their being determined by an employment tribunal:

(a) if asked to do so by both of the parties to the proceedings in question, or

(b) if, in the absence of any such request, the conciliation officer considers that he or she could intervene "with a reasonable prospect of success".

In the case of a dispute that is not yet, but could be, the subject of proceedings before an employment tribunal, a conciliation officer must also act to promote a settlement if asked to do so by either of the parties to that dispute. (*Sources:* TULRA 1992, s.211; ETA 1996, s.18.)

conduct   One of the five permitted reasons for dismissal — the others being capability or qualifications, redundancy, illegality of continued employment or some other substantial reason of a kind that would justify the dismissal of an employee holding the position that the employee held. In proceedings before an employment tribunal on a complaint of unfair dismissal, it is for the respondent employer to show the reason (or principal reason) for the employee's dismissal and to satisfy the tribunal that it was a permitted reason. Once the employer has fulfilled that requirement, the decision as to whether the dismissal was fair or unfair depends on whether, in the circumstances (including the size and administrative resources of the employer's

undertaking) the employer
or unreasonably in treatir
reason for dismissing the en
determined in accordance w
substantial merits of the case.
s.98.)

confidentiality, duty
of

See *fidelity and trust, duty of*. See also *implied term* and *restrictive covenant*.

confinement

See *childbirth*.

constructive
dismissal

There is a constructive dismissal when an employee resigns in circumstances in which he or she is entitled to do so (with or without notice) by reason of the employer's conduct. In *Western Excavating (ECC) Ltd v Sharp* [1978] 2 WLR 344, Lord Denning remarked that "an employee is entitled to treat himself as constructively dismissed if the employer is guilty of conduct which is a significant breach going to the root of the contract of employment, or which shows that the employer no longer intends to be bound by one or more essential terms of the contract".

In *Woods v W M Car Services (Peterborough) Ltd* [1982] IRLR 413, CA, Mr Justice Browne-Wilkinson pointed out that there is an implied term in every contract of employment that an employer will not, without reasonable and proper cause, conduct himself in a manner calculated or likely to destroy or seriously damage the relationship of confidence and trust between employer and employee. Any employer, he said, who persistently attempts to vary an employee's terms and conditions of employment with a view to getting rid of him or her, is in clear breach of that implied duty. Such a breach, he concluded, is a fundamental breach, amounting to a repudiation, since it necessarily goes to the root of the employment contract.

To qualify to pursue a complaint of unfair constructive dismissal before an employment tribunal, an employee must have been continuously employed for one or more years and have been under normal retiring age at the effective date of termination of his or her contract of employment. (*Source:* ERA 1996, ss.95(1)(c), 108 and 109.)

consultations: collective redundancies

Employers proposing to make 100 or more employees redundant at the same establishment within a period of 90 days or less are duty-bound to consult the appropriate representatives about their proposals at least 90 days before the first of the dismissals is to take effect. If fewer that 100 people are to be made redundant at the same establishment within that same 90-day period, consultations must begin at least 30 days before the first of the dismissals takes effect. For these purposes, the "appropriate representatives" are representatives of an independent trade union, if the employees in question are of a description in respect of which the trade union is recognised as having collective bargaining rights; or, if there is no trade union involvement, existing employee representatives or representatives specifically elected by the affected employees to discuss their employer's redundancy proposals.

The consultations must include consultation about ways of avoiding the dismissals, reducing the number of employees to be dismissed, and mitigating the consequence of the dismissals and shall be undertaken by the employer with a view to reaching agreement with the appropriate representatives. Before the consultation process begins, the employer must write to the appropriate representatives disclosing the following:

• the reasons for its proposals

- the number and description of employees it proposes to dismiss as redundant
- the total number of employees at the establishment in question
- the proposed method of selecting the employees who may be dismissed
- the proposed method of carrying out the dismissals (with due regard to any agreed procedure), including the period over which the dismissals are to take effect and
- the proposed method of calculating the amount of any redundancy payments to be made (otherwise than in compliance with a legal obligation to employees who may be dismissed).

On complaint to an employment tribunal, an employer who has either refused or unreasonably failed to consult the appropriate representatives, or failed to disclose the prescribed written information, about its redundancy proposals will be ordered to pay each affected employee an amount not exceeding the equivalent of 90 days' pay.

consultations: safety representatives

Employers planning to introduce working practices, procedures, hazardous substances, plant, machinery or equipment, or any changes in the workplace that may or may not pose a risk to the health, safety and welfare of members of the workforce must consult about their proposals with any trade union-appointed safety representative(s) or (if there is no trade union representation) with any representative of employee safety elected as such by his or her fellow employees to represent their interests in discussions with their employer. In doing so, the employer must disclose to those representatives such information as is necessary to enable them to carry out their official functions and participate fully and effectively in the consultation process. A failure to comply with these (and associated) requirements is a criminal offence for which the penalty on summary conviction is a fine of up to £2000. (*Sources:* **Safety Representatives and Safety Committees Regulations 1977; Health and Safety (Consultation with Employees) Regulations 1996.**)

consultations: transfers of undertakings

An employer contemplating the sale (or transfer) of the whole or part of its business or undertaking, as a going concern, or the purchase of the whole or part of another employer's business or undertaking, is duty-bound to consult the appropriate trade union or employee representatives about the effect the proposed sale or purchase is likely to have on the affected employees. In doing so, the employer must inform them of the reasons for the proposed sale or purchase; when the sale or purchase is to take place, what the legal, economic and social implications will be for the affected employees; what measures (if any) the employer envisages taking in relation to those employees and, if the business or part of the business is being sold, what it knows about the purchaser's intentions in relation to those of its employees who will be transferred with the business (or part of it) when the sale takes place. The consultations must begin long enough before the proposed sale or purchase to enable meaningful discussions to take place, given that those consultations must be conducted with a view to reaching agreement about the impact on the affected employees.

A complaint concerning an employer's failure to consult the appropriate representatives in the circumstances described must be presented to an employment tribunal within three months of the alleged failure. Should the complaint be upheld, the tribunal will make a declaration to that effect and will order the employer to pay each affected employee a sum up to the equivalent of 13 weeks' pay. (*Source:* **Transfer of Undertakings (Protection of Employment) Regulations 1981**.)

continuity of employment

Access to many of the statutory employment rights available to employees under the **Employment Rights Act 1996** and subordinate legislation, is dependent on the employee having completed a prescribed minimum period of continuous service. For example, an employee will not normally qualify to pursue a complaint of unfair dismissal before an employment tribunal unless continuously employed for at least one year at the effective date of termination of his or her contract of employment. Section 212 of the **Employment Rights Act 1996** points out that "any week during the whole or part of which an employee's relations with his employer are governed by a contract of employment counts in computing the employee's period of employment". And again: "An employee's period of continuous employment for the purposes of any provision of this Act begins with the day on which the employee starts work, and ends with the day by reference to which the length of the employee's period of continuous employment is to be ascertained". Some weeks count in computing a period of continuous employment; others do not. The rules are explained in more detail in Part XIV, Chapter 1, of the 1996 Act.

continuous employment

See *continuity of employment*.

contract for services

See *self-employed person*.

contract of employment

"In this Act,'contract of employment' means a contract of service or apprenticeship, whether express or implied, and (if it is express) whether oral or in writing". (*Source:* ERA 1996, s.30(2).) A person engaged under a contract of employment is an employee. A person engaged under a contract that is neither a contract of employment nor a contract for services is said to be employed under a contract *sui generis* (that is to say, of its own kind). For information about the rights of employees and other workers see *employee*.

The traditional litmus test for establishing the existence of a contract of employment (as distinct from a contract for services or a contract *sui generis*) is one of control. If an employer has the right to decide the nature of a worker's duties, and when and how (or, in the case of skilled professionals, the manner in which) those duties are to be carried out, it has been held that the worker is an "employee" and that the contract under which he or she is engaged is a contract of employment. There must also be "mutuality of obligation". In other words, there must be an obligation on the employer to provide paid work and an obligation on the employee to accept and do such work as is offered to him or her on mutually agreed terms and conditions and within specified time limits. An employee can be disciplined or dismissed for failing to turn up for work on time, for failing to carry out his or her duties diligently and efficiently, for disobeying the employer's lawful instructions and so on.

"Under a contract of service (or employment)", remarked Denning LJ in *Stevenson, Jordan and Harrison Ltd v MacDonald and Evans* [1952] 1TLR 101, "a man is employed as part of the business, and his work is done as an integral part of the business; whereas under a contract for services, his work, although done for the business, is not integrated into it but is only accessory to it".

contract of service   See *contract of employment*.

convicted persons   See *Rehabilitation of Offenders Act 1974*.

copyright ownership

In the absence of any specific agreement to the contrary, the copyright in any literary, dramatic or artistic work produced by an employee in the course of his or her employment, and arising out of the duties of that employment, belongs to the employer. (*Source:* **Copyright, Designs and Patents Act 1988**, s.11.)

COT 3 agreement

Named after the form designed for that purpose, a COT 3 agreement is an agreement between an employer and an employee (or other worker), concluded with the intervention of an ACAS-designated conciliation officer, for the resolution of a dispute that is (or could be) the subject of employment tribunal proceedings under s.2(1) of the **Equal Pay Act 1970**; s.63 of the **Sex Discrimination Act 1975**; s.54 of the **Race Relations Act 1976**; ss.64, 68, 86, 137, 138, 146, 168, 169, 170, 174, 188 or 190 of the **Trade Union and Labour Relations (Consolidation) Act 1992**; s.8 of the **Disability Discrimination Act 1995**; ss.8, 13, 15, 18(1), 21(1), 28, 80(1), 92 or 135, or Part V, VI, VII or X of the **Employment Rights Act 1996**; ss.11, 18, 20(1)(a) or 24 of the **National Minimum Wage Act 1998**; regulation 30 of the **Working Time Regulations 1998**; regulation 27 or 42 of the **Transnational Information and Consultation of Employees Regulations 1999**; regulation 5(1) or 7(2) of the **Part-time Workers (Prevention of Less Favourable Treatment) Regulations 2000**; or regulation 3 or 6(2) of the **Fixed-term Employees (Prevention of Less Favourable Treatment) Regulations 2002**.

A COT 3 agreement is a legally-binding agreement. The parties to any such agreement thereby waive their right to bring (or continue with) tribunal proceedings arising out of the dispute or claim to which the agreement relates. In a case where proceedings have already begun and a case number has been allocated, a copy of the agreement will be sent to the Employment Tribunals Service which will acknowledge receipt and direct that all further proceedings in the employee's application be stayed. (*Sources:* TULRA 1992, s.211; ETA 1996, s.18.)

Criminal Records Bureau

An executive agency of the Home Office, the Criminal Records Bureau (CRB) was established under Part V of the **Police Act 1977** to enable registered employers in the public, private and voluntary sectors to identify and (if need be) reject candidates for employment who may be unsuitable for certain work (notably work involving contact with children and other vulnerable members of society) and to provide a speedy service for those persons who are required to disclose particulars of convictions, "spent" or otherwise, when seeking employment in one or other of the occupations or professions listed in the **Rehabilitation of Offenders Act 1974 (Exceptions) Order 1975** (as amended). Employers, voluntary organisations, professional bodies and certain licensing authorities, who have registered with the CRB, may ask successful job applicants to apply to the CRB for one of three types of criminal record checks (CRCs): a Basic Disclosure, a Standard Disclosure or an Enhanced Disclosure. The type of disclosure issued will depend on the nature of the position applied for. Further information concerning the CRB's Disclosure service (how to register, etc) may be accessed and downloaded from websites www.crb.gov.uk and www.disclosure.gov.uk.

D

data protection

Employers and other organisations (banks, insurance companies, credit reference agencies, etc), which maintain or process personal data about any living individual (including employees and other workers) in their computerised or manual filing systems, must ensure that the data in question is processed in accordance with the eight data protection principles laid down in the **Data Protection Act 1998**.

In the employment context, employees and other workers have the right to be informed about any personal data concerning them that is held in their employer's filing systems (computerised or otherwise); and to be given a description of that data and the purposes for which it is being processed, as well as the names or job titles of other persons within the organisation to whom that data is being (or may be) disclosed. Employees have the right also to be provided, on written request (and on payment of a fee of up to £10), with copies of most (if not all) of the data held on their employers' files within the next 40 days. That said, employees do not have the right to see or be provided with copies of any documents on their files that contain information concerning an intended pay rise, or that indicate that they have been earmarked for a transfer, promotion, further training, redundancy or dismissal. Nor does an employer need to disclose the contents of any reference issued by him for employment, education or training purposes. See also *references*.

Employees and other workers also have the right to write to their employers asking them not to process (or to cease processing) personal data about them if that processing has caused (or is likely to cause) substantial and unwarranted damage or distress to them or other persons. In this situation, employers have 21 days within which to write to the employees in question either confirming that they have complied (or intend to comply) with that request, or stating their reasons for non-compliance. Subject to certain transitional provisions (notably in relation to personal data held in manual or paper-based files established before 24 October 1998, for which the transitional period ends on 23 October 2007), employees and other workers may apply to the courts for an order requiring their employers to rectify, block, erase or destroy personal data about them that is inaccurate and any other data containing an expression of opinion about them that is based on that inaccurate data. See also *Information Commissioner*.

Data Protection Act 1998

The rights of employees and other workers to access personal data held on them by their employers in their computerised or manual filing systems, and to ask for the correction or removal of data that is inaccurate or incorrect, are embodied in the **Data Protection Act 1998**, which came into force on 1 March 2000. The Act (which repealed and replaced the eponymous 1984 Act) implements Council Directive 95/46/EC of 24 October 1995 "on the protection of individuals with regard to the processing of personal data and of the free movement of such data". Personal data held (or processed) in manual or paper-based filing systems developed before 24 October 1998 need not comply fully with the 1998 Act until 24 October 2007. During that transitional period, employees will not have the right to apply to the courts for the rectification or destruction of inaccurate personal data held in those paper-based systems. Until 23 October 2007, personal data held in paper-based files developed before 24 October 1998 are exempt for the first data protection principle (except the requirement that the data in question must have been obtained, and be processed, lawfully and fairly) and from the second, third, fourth and fifth data protection principles, see *data protection principles*.

Under the 1984 Act (now repealed) organisations processing personal data about living individuals were required to register that fact with the office of the Data Protection Commissioner (now the Information Commissioner). That system has been replaced by a so-called notification procedure. That said, employers (as data controllers) who process personal data about employees purely for administrative purposes (eg payroll, recruitment, selection, promotion, training, disciplinary matters, etc or for health and safety and other statutory reasons) have no need to notify the Office of the Information Commissioner of that fact. For further information and advice, the reader should either access the Data Protection website on www.dataprotection.gov.uk, or contact the Office of the Information Commissioner on 01625 524510.

data protection principles

The **Data Protection Act 1998** lists eight data protection principles relating to the processing of personal data held on manual or computerised filing systems (ie on an employee's personal file or on any associated or computerised record).

1. The data must have been obtained fairly and lawfully (see above).
2. The data must not be held on file other than for a legitimate purpose (nor be used or made use of for any other purpose).
3. The data must be adequate, relevant and not excessive in relation to the purpose or purposes for which it is kept.
4. The data must be accurate and, where necessary, kept up to date.
5. The data must not be kept for longer than is absolutely necessary.
6. The data must be held in compliance with an employee's rights of access to personal data; must not be processed in a way calculated (or

likely) to cause damage or distress to an employee; and must be corrected, erased or destroyed if inaccurate or no longer relevant.

7. The data must be protected (by the best available means) against unauthorised access or disclosure and against accidental loss, damage or destruction; and must be treated as confidential by the staff to whom it is entrusted.

8. The data must not be transferred to any country or territory (eg to a parent or controlling company in that country or territory) outside the European Economic Area (EEA) whose data protections laws or codes are non-existent or less than adequate — unless the employee agrees, otherwise or the transfer is necessary for employment purposes (eg a proposed transfer or secondment overseas). (*Source:* DPA 1998, ss.4(1) and (2) and Schedule 1.)

deductions from pay

Employers do not have the right to deduct any monies from the wages of any of their workers (or to demand any payment from those workers) unless there is an express term to that effect in each of those workers' contracts specifying the reasons for any such deduction or payment; or unless those workers have each previously agreed in writing to the making of such a deduction or payment. However, this rule does not apply to deductions from a worker's wages in respect of PAYE income tax, National Insurance contributions, the statutory repayment of student loans, or to deductions made in compliance with an attachment of earnings (or maintenance) order imposed by a court of law. Nor does it apply to any overpayment of wages or to any overpayment in respect of expenses incurred by a worker in carrying out his or her employment. Under the common law, workers must nonetheless be informed in writing of their employer's right to recoup any such overpayment either in full or in instalments and to deduct the balance outstanding from the final instalment of wages payable to those workers on the termination of their employment.

The same "prior authorisation" principle applies to workers in retail employment who are contractually liable to deductions from pay (or to demands for payment) in respect of cash shortages or stock deficiencies. However, in these circumstances, the maximum amount that may be deducted from a worker's wages in respect of one or more shortages or deficiencies may not exceed one-tenth of the gross amount of the wages payable to the worker on that day.

A complaint that an employer has made unlawful deductions from a worker's wages, or has demanded and received unauthorised payments, may be referred to an employment tribunal. If the complaint is upheld, the employer will be ordered to make restitution. (*Source:* ERA 1996, Part II.)

dependant, meaning of

In relation to an employee, a "dependant" means a spouse, a child, a parent, a person who lives in the same household as the employee (otherwise than by reason of being his employee, tenant, lodger or boarder). The term also includes any person (such as grandparent, aunt or uncle) who reasonably relies on the employee for assistance on an occasion when the person falls ill or is injured or assaulted, or to make arrangements for the provision of care in the event of illness or injury. (*Source:* ERA 1996, s.57A(3) and (4).)

dependants, time off for

Every employee, regardless of his or her age, working hours, or length of service, has the legal right to a reasonable amount of unpaid time off work in the following circumstances:

- when the employee's wife or partner is having a baby
- when a dependant is suddenly taken ill, or has been injured or assaulted
- when a dependant dies (eg making funeral arrangements and/or attending the funeral)
- to make alternative arrangements when existing arrangements for the care of a dependant have unexpectedly come to an end or been disrupted
- to act when the employee's child is involved in an incident at school. (*Source:* ERA 1996, s.57A and B). See also *dependant, meaning of.*

detrimental treatment

An employee has the right not to be victimised, punished or subjected to any other detriment by any act, or any deliberate failure to act, by his or her employer:

- for performing (or proposing to perform) his or her functions as a safety representative, a member of a safety committee, a representative of employee safety, or a "competent person" (designated as such to advise on procedures for reducing risks to health and safety)
- for calling attention to circumstances connected with his or her work which were reasonably believed to be harmful or potentially harmful to health or safety; or (in the absence of any safety representative or safety committee) for leaving the workplace in circumstances of danger which were reasonably believed to be serious and imminent (or for refusing to return while the danger persisted)
- or (as a protected or opted-out shop worker or betting worker) for refusing (or proposing to refuse) to do shop work or betting work on a Sunday (or on a particular Sunday)

- for challenging an alleged infringement of (or refusing to forego) his or her rights under the **Working Time Regulations 1998**
- for performing or proposing to perform his or her functions as a pension scheme trustee or employee representative
- (as a young person) for exercising his or her rights to time off work for study or training
- (as a worker) for having made a protected disclosure
- for performing or for exercising her statutory rights in relation to pregnancy, childbirth or maternity
- for taking (or being entitled to) parental leave, paternity leave, maternity leave, adoption leave or time off for dependants.

(*Source:* ERA 1996, Part V.)

direct discrimination

Under the **Sex Discrimination Act 1975**, the **Race Relations Act 1976**, and the **Disability Discrimination Act 1995**, employers are *prima facie* guilty of unlawful direct discrimination if they refuse to interview or employ any person; or deny equal opportunities for promotion, transfer, training, or equal access to benefits, facilities or services to any person; or dismiss a person or subject a person to any detriment on grounds of sex, marital status, pregnancy, gender reassignment, race, colour, nationality, ethnic or national origins, nationality or disability. Employers are also liable under those acts if they instruct any person (manager, supervisor, employment agency, etc) to discriminate on such grounds. There is no upper limit on the amount of compensation that may be awarded by the employment tribunals in such cases. It is likewise unlawful for an employer to refuse to employ (or interview) any person because he or she is, or is not, a member of a trade union, or because he or she is unwilling to accept a requirement to take steps to become or cease to be, or remain or not to become, a member of a trade union, or to make payments or suffer deductions in the event of his or her not being a member of a trade union. (*Sources:* SDA 1975, s.6; RRA 1976, s.4; DDA 1995, s.4; TULRA 1992, s.137.) See also *indirect discrimination* and *genuine occupational qualification.*

disability

A person has a disability for the purposes of the **Disability Discrimination Act 1995** if he or she has a physical or mental impairment which has a substantial and long-term effect on his or her ability to carry out normal day-to-day activities. The expression "mental impairment'" includes an impairment resulting from, or consisting of, a mental illness if, but only if, the illness is a well-recognised clinical illness. The effect of an impairment is a long-term effect if it has lasted (or is likely to last) for at least 12 months; or it is likely to last for the rest of the affected person's life.

Where an impairment ceases to have a substantial adverse effect on a person's ability to carry out normal day-to-day activities, it is to be treated as continuing to have that effect if that effect is likely to recur. An impairment that consists of a severe disfigurement is to be treated as having a substantial adverse effect on the ability of the person concerned to carry out normal day-to-day activities. However, a severe disfigurement consisting of a tattoo that has not been removed or a body piercing carried out for decorative or other non-medical purposes (including any object attached to any such piercing) is not to be treated as a severe disfigurement for the purposes of the 1995 Act. (*Sources:* DDA 1996, s.1 and Schedule 1; **Disability Discrimination (Meaning of Disability) Regulations 1996**, regulation 5.)

Where a person has a progressive condition (such as cancer, multiple sclerosis or muscular dystrophy, or infection by the human immunodeficiency virus (HIV) and, as a result of that condition, he or she has an impairment which has (or has had) an effect on his or her ability to carry out normal day-to-day activities, but that effect is (or was) not a substantial adverse effect, he or she shall be taken to have an impairment which has such a substantial adverse effect if the condition is likely to result in his or her having such an impairment. (*Source:* DDA 1995, Schedule 1.)

An impairment that is likely to have a substantial adverse effect on a person's ability to carry out normal day-to-day activities, but for the fact that the person concerned is receiving medical treatment or has been issued or fitted with a prosthesis or other aid, is nonetheless to be treated as having that effect. However, this does not apply to a person with impaired sight if that impairment is correctable by spectacles or contact lenses or by some other prescribed means (*Source*: DDA 1995, Schedule 1.)

Under the **Disability Discrimination (Meaning of Disability) Regulations 1996**, addiction to alcohol, nicotine or any other substance is not to treated as amounting to an impairment for the purposes of the 1995 Act (unless the addiction originally resulted from the administration of medically-prescribed drugs or other medical treatment). Other conditions not to be treated as impairments include a tendency to steal or set fires, a tendency to the physical or sexual abuse of other persons, exhibitionism and voyeurism. Nor is the condition known as seasonal allergic rhinitis (or hay fever) to be treated as mounting to an impairment unless it aggravates the effect of another condition (**Disability Discrimination (Meaning of Disability) Regulations 1996**, regulations 3 and 4).

disability discrimination

For the purposes of the **Disability Discrimination Act 1995** (DDA), "an employer discriminates against a disabled person if:

(a) for a reason which relates to the disabled person's disability, he treats him less favourably than he treats or would treat others to whom that reason does not or would not apply; and

(b) he cannot show that the treatment in question is justified.

Such less favourable treatment can be justified if, but only if, the reason for it is both material to the circumstances of the particular case and substantial" (DDA, s.5(1) and (3)). "An employer also discriminates against a disabled person if (a) he fails to comply with a s.6 duty imposed on him in relation to the disabled person, and he cannot show that the failure to comply with that duty is justified". A failure to comply with a s.6 duty is justified if, but only if, the reason for the failure is both material to the circumstances of the particular case and substantial (DDA, s.5(2) and (4)).

For the above purposes, less favourable treatment is to be taken to be justified "if it results from applying to the disabled person a term or practice:

(a) under which the amount of a person's pay is wholly or partly dependent on that person's performance; and

(b) which is applied to all the employer's employees or to all of a class of his employees which includes the disabled person, but which is not defined by reference to any disability".

Disability Discrimination Act 1995

Under the 1995 Act, most of whose provisions came into force on 8 November 1995, it is unlawful to discriminate against disabled persons in connection with employment, the provision of goods, facilities and services or the disposal or management of premises.

Disability Rights Commission

Established under the **Disability Rights Commission Act 1999**, the Disability Rights Commission (DRC) has functions and powers similar to those available to, and exercised by, the Equal Opportunities Commission (EOC) and the Commission for Racial Equality (CRE), ie to conduct formal investigations, issue non-discrimination notices, deal with persistent instances of disability discrimination, provide assistance to disabled persons in relation to any proceedings before a tribunal or court and issue codes of practice.

disabled person

A disabled person is a person who has a disability within the meaning of the **Disability Discrimination Act 1995** (s.1).

disciplinary and grievance procedures

In companies, firms or businesses with 20 or more people on the payroll (including employees employed by any associated employer), the written statement of employment particulars issued to every new employee must include a note specifying any disciplinary rules applicable to the employee, or referring the employee to a document specifying such rules which should be accessible to the employee. The note should also give the name or job title of a person to whom the employee can apply if dissatisfied with any disciplinary decision relating to him or her. If there are any further steps or procedures involved in such an application, the note must explain those steps or refer the employee to another document, such as a staff handbook, that explains them in detail. ACAS Code of Practice 1 on *Disciplinary and Grievance Procedures* provides practical guidance for employers on the development and promotion of disciplinary rules and procedures. Copies of the Code are available from ACAS Reader Limited on 0870 242 9090.

disclosure of information

Current employment legislation imposes a duty on employers (in a variety of circumstances) to disclose specified information about their business activities, policies and plans:

- to trade union representatives for the purposes of collective bargaining (*Source:* TULRA 1992, s.181)
- to the appropriate representatives (and to the Secretary of State for Trade and Industry) when contemplating collective redundancies (*Source:* TULRA 1992, ss.188-198)
- to the appropriate representatives when contemplating the sale or transfer of their businesses (or discrete parts of those businesses) or the purchase of the whole or part of another employer's business (*Source:* TUPE 1981, regulations 10-11A)
- to safety representatives and representatives of employee safety (*Sources:* **Safety Representatives and Safety Committees Regulations 1977**, regulation 7; and the **Health and Safety (Consultations with Employees) Regulations 1996**)
- to "competent persons" designated as such to advise on health and safety issues within the workplace (*Source:* **Management of Health and Safety at Work Regulations 1999**, regulation 7)
- to any worker who believes that he or she is not being paid the correct national minimum wage (ie by providing access to the worker's payroll records) (*Source:* NMWA 1998, s.11)
- to members of Special Negotiating Bodies (SNBs) and European Works Councils (EWCs)

(*Source:* **Transnational Information and Consultation of Employees Regulations 1999** (TICER))

- (in a company employing 250 or more people) to shareholders, employees and the public at large concerning the company's policy and arrangements for the employment of disabled persons (*Source:* **Companies Act 1985**, Schedule 7, paragragh 9).

An employer's failure to comply with these "disclosure" requirements may prompt complaints to the employment tribunals, prosecution or the intervention of the relevant enforcing authorities (eg the Health and Safety Inspectorate or Inland Revenue enforcing officers), awards of compensation or fines.

dismissal, meaning of	An employee is dismissed by his or her employer if, and only if:

- the contract under which he or she is employed is terminated by the employer (whether with or without notice)
- he or she is employed under a limited-term contract and that contract terminates by virtue of the limiting event without being renewed under the same contract
- the employee terminates the contract under which he or she is employed (with or without notice) in circumstances in which he or she is entitled to terminate it by reason of the employer's conduct.

An employee shall also be taken to have been dismissed by his or her employer if the employer gives notice to terminate the contract of employment and, at a time within the period of that notice, the employee gives notice to the employer to terminate the contract on a date earlier than the date on which the employer's notice is due to expire; and the reason for the dismissal is the reason for which the employer's notice is given. (*Source:* ERA 1996. s.95.)

dismissal procedures agreement

An agreement between an employer and one or more independent trade unions which, once designated (ie approved) by order of the Secretary of State for Trade and Industry substitutes for the right of an employee under s.94 of the **Employment Rights Act 1996** to pursue a complaint of unfair dismissal before an employment tribunal. The agreement will not be so designated unless it provides for procedures to be followed in cases where an employee claims that he or she has been, or is in the course of being, unfairly dismissed; unless those procedures are available without discrimination to all employees covered by the agreement; and unless the remedies for unfair dismissal provided by the agreement are on the whole as beneficial as (but not necessarily identical with those provided under the 1996 Act). The agreement must also include provision for arbitration when a decision cannot be reached concerning the fairness or otherwise of an employee's dismissal or if there is a disagreement between the parties on a question of law arising out of such a decision. Finally, the provisions of the agreement must be such that it can be determined with reasonable certainty whether or not a particular employee is one to whom the agreement applies. If a designated dismissal procedures agreement applies only to certain types of dismissal (eg a dismissal on grounds of misconduct) it cannot be employed to assess the fairness of dismissals for other reasons. The evidence is that, to date, very few such agreements have either been presented to, or approved, by order of the Secretary of State. (*Source:* ERA 1996, s.110.)

display screen equipment

Legislation concerning the ergonomic design and use of display screen equipment (VDUs) and associated workstations is to be found in the **Health and Safety (Display Screen Equipment) Regulations 1992**. Those Regulations were amended on 17 September 2002, by the **Health and Safety at Work (Miscellaneous Amendments) Regulations 2002** by removing, in relation to workstations, differences in treatment between "users" and "operators". Under the 1992 Regulations (as amended), employers must assess the risk to which employees and other workers may be exposed while operating such equipment; take appropriate steps to eliminate or minimise those risks; ensure that the design and accessibility of VDU workstations meet minimum statutory requirements; organise the work of VDU users in such a way as to enable them to take regular breaks or changes of activity; and, on request, arrange and pay for initial and repeat eye and eyesight tests and pay for special corrective spectacles (if so prescribed by an optometrist or doctor). A booklet entitled *Display Screen Equipment Work* (Ref. L26), providing guidance on the Regulations and workplace assessments is available from HSE Books on 01787 881165.

E

effective date of termination

A complaint of unfair or unlawful dismissal must be presented to an employment tribunal within three months of the effective date of termination of the employee's contract of employment. In the case of an employee whose contract is terminated with notice, whether given by the employer or by the employee himself (or herself), it is the date on which that notice expires. If the employee's contract is terminated without notice, it is the date on which the dismissal takes place. If a limited-term contract terminates by virtue of the limiting event (without being renewed under the same contract), it is the date on which the termination takes effect. (*Source:* ERA 1996, s.97(1).)

However, a different formula is applied when determining whether an employee claiming unfair dismissal has the qualifying period of employment needed to pursue such a complaint (ie one year ending with the effective date of termination). If such an employee has been summarily dismissed (ie without notice, or with less notice than that prescribed by s.86 of the **Employment Rights Act 1996**), the effective date of termination of his or her contract of employment is the date on which the statutory minimum period of notice would have expired had it been given on the date the dismissal occurred. The same rule applies if the employee has resigned without notice in circumstances in which he or she is entitled to do so by virtue of the employer's conduct (ie a constructive dismissal). An employment tribunal will adopt the same formula when determining the amount of any basic award of compensation for unfair dismissal. (*Source:* ERA 1996, s.97 (2) and (4).)

An employee's right to a redundancy payment is likewise determined by reference to his or her length of continuous service at the effective date of termination of his or her contract of employment. An employee with less than two years' service at that time (excluding any period of employment before the age of 18) is not entitled to a redundancy payment when his or her employment comes to an end. If a redundant employee is dismissed without notice (or with less notice than that prescribed by s.86 of the 1996 Act) the effective date of termination of his or her contract of employment (ie the relevant date for redundancy payment purposes) is the date on which that statutory minimum period of notice would have expired had it been given on the date on which the employee was peremptorily dismissed (or dismissed with less notice than that prescribed by law. (*Source:* ERA 1996, s.145.)

employee   A person who works (or, where the employment has ended, worked) under a contract of employment (or a contract of service or apprenticeship). A self-employed person, on the other hand, is a person who is in business on his or her own account, and is engaged by a client or customer under a contract for services. A worker who is neither an employee nor a self-employed person is said to be engaged under a contract *sui generis* (that is to say, of its own kind). The latter category usually applies to casual or occasional workers (perhaps drawn from a pool of workers who may or may not be available for work at short notice) who are engaged on an "as and when required" basis and who are free, without penalty, to accept or reject any offer of work made to them and to come and go as they please.

Understanding the distinction between workers who are "employees" and those who are not is important. Workers who are employees have qualified access to most (if not all) of the statutory employment rights laid down in legislation such as the **Trade Union and Labour Relations (Consolidation) Act 1992** and the **Employment Rights Act 1996**. Workers who are neither employees nor self-employed persons nonetheless enjoy the protection afforded by legislation such as the **National Minimum Wage Act 1998**, the **Working Time Regulations 1998**, the **Part-time Workers (Prevention of Less Favourable Treatment) Regulations 2000**, and Part IVA of the **Employment Rights Act 1996 (Protected Disclosures)**. They also share the right not to be discriminated against on grounds of sex, race or disability. Where there is a dispute concerning the true nature of a worker's contractual relationship with an employer, the issue will, as always, be resolved by the tribunals and courts.

employee representatives, time off for

See *time off work: general*.

employer

The term "employer", in relation to an employee or a worker, means the person by whom the employee or worker is (or, where the employment has ceased, was) employed. (*Source:* ERA 1996, s.230(4).)

employers' association

An organisation of employers or individual owners of undertakings whose principal purposes include the regulation of relations between employers and workers or trade unions; or which consists of constituent or affiliated organisations which fulfil these conditions or representatives of such constituent or affiliated organisations, whose principal purposes include the regulation of relations between employers and workers or between employers and trade unions, or the regulation of relations between its constituent or affiliated organisations. (*Source:* TULRA 1992, s.122; ERA 1996, s.235(1).)

A list containing the names of employers' associations is maintained by the Certification Officer. The list is open for public inspection at all reasonable hours, free of charge. An organisation of employers, whenever formed, whose name is not entered on the list of employers' associations may apply to the Certification Officer to have its name entered on the list. The obligations of employers' association and restrictions on their activities are to be found in Part II of the **Trade Union and Labour Relations Act 1992**.

employment

In relation to an employee, "employment" means employment under a contract of employment and, in relation to a worker, it means employment under his or her contract. However, the Secretary of State for Trade and Industry may by regulations provide that, subject to any prescribed exceptions and modifications, access to the provisions of the **Employment Rights Act 1996** will extend to any employment under which secondary Class 1 contributions are payable under Part I of the **Social Security Contributions and Benefits Act 1992**, but which is not employment under a contract of service or of apprenticeship (ie a contract of employment). (*Source:* ERA 1996, ss.171 and 235(5).)

employment agencies and businesses

An "employment agency" is essentially a recruitment agency that is in business to find permanent employment for workers, and permanent workers for employers. When publishing advertisements, an employment agency must make it clear that it is an employment agency acting on behalf of one or more (albeit unnamed) employers. An "employment business" (or temporary staff agency), on the other hand, usually recruits its own workers or has a number of workers on standby, hiring them out to client employers on a temporary basis. Employment businesses are commonly associated with the supply of "temp" secretaries, clerical staff, drivers, etc. The activities of employment agencies and businesses are presently regulated by the **Conduct of Employment Agencies and Employment Businesses Regulations 1976** (made under the **Employment Agencies Act 1973**). Employers seeking advice on their dealings with employment agencies and businesses may contact the Employment Agencies Standards Office on 08459 555105.

The 1976 Regulations are soon to be revoked. Following an initial consultation period, the DTI published a final draft consultation document on 23 July 2002, accompanied by draft new **Conduct of Employment Agencies and Employment Businesses Regulations 1976**, designed to further regulate the activities of employment agencies and businesses (notably in relation to the supply of "suitable" temporary workers). Under the new legislation, employment businesses will be obliged (amongst other things) to inform the client employer whether the "temps" they supply are employed by the agency itself (eg under contracts of service or employment) or whether they are self-employed.

The new Regulations are also intended resolve the vexed issue of "temp to perm" fees. Once those Regulations come into force, client employers seeking to take agency temps into their direct employment may either agree to pay a reasonable "temp to perm" fee or (in the absence of any such agreement) serve notice on the agency that they propose to extend the hiring arrangement — either for a further eight weeks (commencing on the day after the day on which the contract between the employer and the agency for the supply of the temp in question came to an end) or for the period of 14 weeks commencing on the first day on which the temp started work with the client employer under that contract, whichever of those periods ends later, discounting any break of more than six weeks between the end of one hire contract and the beginning of the next — at the end of which time no further fee would be payable. The new Regulations (once approved) are expected to come into force in mid to late 2003. Copies of the consultation document and the accompanying draft Regulations may be accessed and downloaded from the Department of Trade and Industry's website www.dti.gov.uk/er/agency/newregs.htm.

Employment Appeal Tribunal

An appeal lies to the Employment Appeal Tribunal (EAT) on any question of law arising from any decision of (or arising in any proceedings before) an employment tribunal under the relevant legislation (see list in *employment tribunal*).

The procedure for appeals to the EAT is to be found in the Employment Appeal Tribunal Rules 1993 (as amended).

An organisation aggrieved by the refusal of the Certification Officer to enter its name in the list of trade unions and employers' associations (or by his or her decision to remove its name from that list) may also appeal to the EAT, as may a trade union aggrieved by the refusal of the Certification Officer to issue it with a certificate of independence (or by his or her decision to withdraw its certificate). The rights of appeal in these circumstances extend to any question of fact or law arising in the proceedings before, or arising from the decision of, the Certification Officer. (*Source:* TULRA 1992, ss.9, 56A and 126.)

Proceedings before the EAT are presided over by a High Court judge or by a Court of Appeal judge accompanied by two or four appointed members, so that employers and workers are equally represented. With the consent of the parties to the appeal, proceedings before the EAT may be heard by a judge and one appointed member, or by a judge and three appointed members. However, appeal proceedings on a question arising from any decision of (or arising in any proceedings before) an employment tribunal — which consisted of a tribunal chairman sitting alone — shall be heard by a judge sitting alone, unless a judge directs that the appeal proceedings should be heard by a judge and one or three appointed members. (*Source:* ETA 1996, ss.22 and 28.) Appeals against the judgments of the EAT lie to the Court of Appeal, on a point of law only.

employment business

See *employment agencies and businesses*.

employment contract

See *contract of employment* and *employee*.

employment tribunal

First established under the **Industrial Training Act 1964** to hear employers' appeals against the imposition of industrial training levies, the jurisdiction of the employment tribunals (or industrial tribunals, as they are still known in Northern Ireland) has long since been expanded to encompass references, claims or complaints arising out any alleged infringement of an employee's (or other worker's) statutory rights under:

- the **Equal Pay Act 1970**
- the **Sex Discrimination Act 1975**
- the **Race Relations Act 1976**
- the **Trade Union and Labour Relations (Consolidation) Act 1992**
- the **Disability Discrimination Act 1995**
- the **Employment Rights Act 1996**
- the **Employment Tribunals Act 1996**
- the **National Minimum Wage Act 1998**
- the **Tax Credits Act 2002**
- the **Working Time Regulations 1998**
- the **Transnational Information and Consultation of Employees Regulations 1999**
- the **Part-time Workers (Prevention of Less Favourable Treatment) Regulations 2000**
- the **Fixed-term Employees (Prevention of Less Favourable Treatment) Regulations 2002**. (*Source:* ETA 1996, s.21.)

The employment tribunals also have jurisdiction to entertain wrongful dismissal and other breach of contract claims that arise or remain outstanding on the termination of an employee's contract of employment (save for claims for damages in excess of £25,000). However, they do not have jurisdiction to entertain personal injury claims, or claims relating to tied accommodation, intellectual property, obligations of confidence, and restrictive covenants. (*Sources:* **Employment Tribunals Extension of Jurisdiction (England and Wales) Order 1994**; and the **Employment Tribunals Extension of Jurisdiction (Scotland) Order 1994**.)

A complaint or reference to an employment tribunal is commenced when the complainant employee (or worker) completes and submits an originating application (Form IT1) to the nearest regional office of the Employment Tribunals Service. A copy of that document (once registered) is sent to the respondent employer and to ACAS (which latter may intervene at the request of both parties to the dispute with a view to promoting an "out of court" settlement). The employer will also be sent a Notice of Appearance (Form IT3) which should be completed and returned to the Secretary to the Tribunals within the next 21 days. Tribunal hearings are usually conducted by a chairman (a barrister or solicitor of at least seven years' standing) accompanied by two lay members (each with relevant experience in industrial relations matters) or (in prescribed circumstances) by a chairman sitting alone.

For further information, contact the Employment Tribunals Service Enquiry Line on 0845 795 9775 (for copies of the following free booklets: *What to do if taken to a tribunal* and *Hearings at the employment tribunals*) or visit the website www.employmenttribunals.gov.uk.

An appeal from the decision of an employment tribunal (on a point of law only) lies to the Employment Appeal Tribunal (EAT). The appeal must be lodged within 42 days of the date on which the full written decision was sent to the employer or employee. The relevant legislation is to be found in the **Employment Tribunals (Constitution and Rules of Procedure) Regulations 2001**; the **Employment Tribunals (Constitution and Rules of Procedure) (Scotland) Regulations 2001**; and the Employment Appeal Tribunal Rules 1993.

Equal Opportunities Commission

Established under s.53 of (and Schedule 3 to) the **Sex Discrimination Act 1975**, the Equal Opportunities Commission (EOC) comprises a minimum of eight (but no more than 15) commissioners, appointed on a full-time or part-time basis: to work towards the elimination of discrimination between the sexes; to promote equality of opportunity between men and women generally; to promote equality of opportunity in the fields of employment and vocational training for persons who intend to undergo, are undergoing or have undergone gender reassignment; and to keep under review the working of the 1975 Act, the **Equal Pay Act 1970** and discriminatory provisions in health and safety legislation and, when so required by the Secretary of State, or otherwise thought necessary, to draw up and submit to the Secretary of State proposals for amending that legislation. The EOC may issue codes of practice, conduct formal investigations, serve non-discrimination notices, provide help and advice to persons pursuing complaints of unlawful discrimination, and apply to the courts for injunctions or orders designed to restrain the activities of persistent offenders. (*Source:* SDA 1975, Part VI and Schedule 3.) See also *equal pay* and *sex discrimination.*

equal pay
Section 1 of the **Equal Pay Act 1970** points out that, if the contract under which a woman (of whatever age) is employed at an establishment in Great Britain does not include an equality clause (directly or by reference to a collective agreement) it shall be deemed to include one. In short (by virtue of that implied contractual term), a woman employed on like work with a man in the same employment, or work rated as equivalent, or work of equal value, must be paid the same as that man (or be on the same incremental pay scale, if pay is determined by reference to qualifications, experience or length of service and not the gender of the person doing the work in question) and must enjoy the same terms and conditions of employment. However, an equality clause does not operate in relation to terms affected by compliance with laws regulating the employment of women, or affording special treatment to women in connection with pregnancy or confinement.

Any claim in respect of the contravention of a woman's rights under the 1970 Act (or those of man), including a claim for arrears of remuneration or damages in respect of that contravention, may be presented by way of a complaint to an employment tribunal. The complaint must be presented within six months of the alleged infringement or, if the woman or man is no longer employed by the same or an associated employer, within six months of the date on which his or her employment came to an end. If such a complaint is upheld, the tribunal may award the complainant arrears of compensation backdated for a period of up to two years. However, following a referral to, and the subsequent decision of, the European Court of Justice (ECJ), the EAT in *Levez v T H Jennings (Harlow Pools) Ltd (No. 2)* [1999] IRLR 764 held that the limit on the arrears of remuneration laid down in the 1970 Act was incompatible with Community law and concluded that claims for arrears of remuneration could relate to the period of six years (not two years) immediately preceding the commencement of the claim. See also *Equal Pay Act 1970*.

Equal Pay Act 1970   The **Equal Pay Act 1970** which received the Royal Assent on 29 May 1970, and came into force in Great Britain on 29 December 1975, imposes the requirement of equal treatment for men and women in the same employment. Under the 1970 Act, any contract under which a woman (or man) is employed is deemed to include an equality clause. What this means is that a woman employed on like work with a man in the same employment, or work rated as equivalent, or work of equal value, must be paid the same as that man and be employed under the same terms and conditions as that man. However, an equality clause does not operate in relation to a variation between the woman's contract and the man's contract if the employer proves that the variation is genuinely due to a material factor that is not gender-related. The 1970 Act applies equally to a man who may likewise compare the terms and conditions under which he is employed with those enjoyed by a woman in the same employment.

For the purposes of the 1970 Act, the word "employed" means employed under a contract of service or apprenticeship (ie a contract of employment) or a contract personally to execute any work or labour.

equal value, work of   See *work rated as equivalent*.

equality clause   see *Equal Pay Act 1970*.

EU directives   The Council of the European Communities issues so-called "directives" to EU Member States after considering proposals from the Commission, the opinion of the European Parliament and the views of the Economic and Social Committee. Each Member State must integrate those directives into its domestic legislation within the time limits (usually one to three years) prescribed by the directives themselves. Many such directives have already been incorporated into UK law, mostly in the form of statutory regulations and orders.

European Convention on Human Rights   Signed in Rome on 4 November 1950, and entered into force on 3 September 1953, the European Convention on Human Rights and Fundamental Freedoms was imported into UK legislation by the **Human Rights Act 1998**, which came into force on 2 October 2000. Under the (relevant) Articles of the Convention:

- "No one shall be held in slavery or servitude. No one shall be required to perform forced or compulsory labour" (Article 4).
- "Everyone has the right to respect for his private and family life, his home and his correspondence" (Article 8).
- "Everyone has the right to freedom of thought, conscience and religion; this right includes freedom to change his religion or belief and freedom, either alone or in community with others and in public or private, to manifest his religion or belief, in worship, teaching, practice and observance" (Article 9).
- "Everyone has the right to freedom of expression" (Article 10).
- "Everyone has the right to freedom of peaceful assembly and to freedom of association with

others, including the right to form and to join trade unions for the protection of his interests" (Article 11).

- "The enjoyment of the rights and freedoms set forth in this Convention shall be secured without discrimination on any grounds such as sex, race, colour, language, religion, political or other opinion, national or social origin, association with a national minority, property, birth or other status" (Article 14).

The European Commission on Human Rights and the European Court of Human Rights (ECHR) were established under the Convention to ensure the observance of the engagements undertaken by the High Contracting Parties (Article 19).

European Court of Human Rights

Established under Articles 19 and 38 of the European Convention on Human Rights, the European Court of Human Rights (ECHR) consists of a number of judges (each elected for a period of nine years) equal to that of the Members of the Council of Europe. The Court is presided over by a President and Vice-President (elected by the Court) who each hold office for three years. No two judges may be nationals of the same State. The jurisdiction of the Court extends to all cases concerning the interpretation and application of the Convention referred to it by the signatory States or by the European Commission on Human Rights ("the Commission"). The Court's judgment is final. Although an individual litigant has access to the ECHR, his or her claim must first be lodged with the Commission to ensure that it is admissible, ie admissible in the sense that all domestic remedies have been exhausted, that proceedings have been initiated within six months of the final adjudication in a UK court and that it relates to a right guaranteed by the Convention.

European Court of Justice (ECJ)

Consisting of 15 judges (ie one from each of the 15 EU Member States), and assisted by six Advocates-General), the function of the European Court of Justice (ECJ) is to ensure that Member States comply with their obligations under the Treaty of Rome and correctly implement, interpret and apply binding EU legislation (ie directives and regulations). The ECJ will only entertain claims referred to it by one of a Member State's own judicial bodies or by a judge seeking an interpretation of community law to enable him or her to give a judgment in a case before him. The ECJ adjudicates only on the interpretation of the Treaty, leaving it to the relevant Member State's domestic courts to apply that interpretation to a particular case. On completion of certain formalities, the European Commission may permit an individual to present a claim before the ECJ.

European Economic Area

The European Economic Area (EEA) comprises Austria, Belgium, Denmark, Finland, France, Germany, Greece, Iceland, the Republic of Ireland, Italy, Liechtenstein, Luxembourg, the Netherlands, Norway, Portugal, Spain, Sweden and the UK. Nationals of those countries have the right of entry and residence in the UK and the concomitant right to take up employment in the UK without the need for work permits. The same is also true of Swiss nationals (although Switzerland is not a member of the EEA) (*Source:* **Immigration (European Economic Area) Regulations 2000**, as amended by the **Immigration (Swiss Free Movement of Persons) (No.3) Regulations 2002**). See also *work permits*.

European Union

The European Union (or EU) comprises Austria, Belgium, Denmark, Finland, France, Germany, Greece, the Irish Republic, Italy, Luxembourg,

The Netherlands, Spain, Sweden, Portugal and the UK. See also *EU directives*.

European Works Councils (EWCs)

UK-based multinational companies with 1000 or more employees "on the payroll" (of whom 150 or more are employed in each of at least two EEA Member States) must respond positively to a valid request for the establishment of a European Works Council (EWC) or for a European-level "information and consultation procedure". This requirement (with accompanying rules and procedures) is to be found in the **Transnational Information and Consultation of Employees Regulations 1999** implementing Council Directive 94/45/EC "on the establishment of a European Works Council or a procedure in Community-scale undertakings and Community-scale groups of undertakings for the purposes of informing and consulting employees". The Regulations came into force in the UK on 15 January 2000.

expected week of childbirth

Means the week, beginning on Sunday and ending at midnight on the following Saturday, in which it is expected that childbirth will occur. It is the expected week of childbirth (EWC) that determines the earliest date on which a pregnant employee may begin her ordinary maternity leave, not to mention her right (if any) to statutory maternity pay (SMP) and additional maternity leave. See also *certificate of expected confinement* and *paternity leave*. (*Source:* ERA 1996, s.235.)

express terms

These are terms specifically agreed between the parties to a contract of employment. Express terms include those laid down in letters of offer and in the written statement of employment particulars (necessarily issued to every new recruit within two months of the date on which he or she starts work) and in documents (such as staff or works handbooks, policy documents, job descriptions, and the like) which explain those particulars in more detail. They are also to be found in the terms of a collective or workforce agreement, and in disciplinary rules and procedures (and grievance procedures) imported into an employee's contract of employment.

F

Fair Employment and Treatment (Northern Ireland) Order 1998

Under the 1998 Order it is unlawful for employers in Northern Ireland to discriminate against job applicants and existing employees because of their political opinions or religious beliefs. Any person who is discriminated against in this way may complain to the Fair Employment Tribunal and will be awarded substantial compensation if his or her complaint is upheld. There is no upper limit on the amount of compensation that may be awarded in such cases.

Every employer in Northern Ireland with more than 10 employees on the payroll (excluding part-timers working fewer than 16 hours a week) must register with the Equality Commission for Northern Ireland (formerly known as the Fair Employment Commission) and must submit annual "monitoring returns" to the Commission. A failure to comply with these requirements is a criminal offence for which the penalty on summary conviction is a fine of up to £5000, plus a further fine of up to £500 per day for each day of continued non-compliance.

family friendly rights

The qualified rights of eligible employees to maternity leave and pay, adoption leave and pay, unpaid parental leave and paid paternity leave, and the right of parents of children under the age of six (or under the age of 18, in the case of a

71

disabled child) to apply for more flexible working arrangements, are collectively referred to as "family friendly rights".

family life, respect for

The right of everyone (including an employee or other worker) "to respect for his private and family life, his home and his correspondence" (Article 8 of the European Convention on Human Rights).

fidelity and trust, duty of

The implied contractual duty of every employee to serve his or her employer honestly and faithfully and not to do anything calculated to damage or otherwise undermine his employer's reputation or business interests (eg by misusing, communicating or divulging to unauthorised third parties sensitive or confidential information relating to his or her employer's business affairs, pricing policy, marketing strategies, processes or trade secrets). The employee's duty of confidentiality persists after the employment relationship has come to an end. See also *implied term* and *restrictive covenant*.

fixed-term contract

"A contract of employment or service that terminates on the expiry of a specific term, on the completion of a particular task, or on the occurrence or non-occurrence of any other specific event (other than the attainment by the employee of his normal and bona fide retiring age in the establishment for an employee holding the position held by him)." (*Source:* FTER 2002, regulation 1(2).)

fixed-term employee

This is an employee who is employed under a fixed-term contract (that is to say, under a contract of employment) that terminates on the expiry of a specific term, or on completion of a specific task, or on the occurrence or non-occurrence of any other specific event (other than the attainment by the employee of any normal and bona fide retiring age). Under the

Fixed-term Employees (Prevention of Less Favourable Treatment) Regulations 2002, which came into force on 1 October 2002, employees working under fixed-term or task-related contracts (for however long or short a period) must not be treated less favourably than comparable permanent employees working at the same establishment. Fixed-term employees must also be afforded the right to apply for permanent jobs within the employing organisation and must be informed of all suitable vacancies when and as they arise. Furthermore, they now enjoy access to a number of statutory rights previously denied to them under the **Employment Rights Act 1996** and related legislation, including the right to be paid statutory sick pay (SSP) when incapacitated for work through illness or injury. (*Source:* **Fixed-term Employees (Prevention of Less Favourable Treatment) Regulations 2002**.)

flexible working
From 6 April 2003, eligible employees who are the parents (or adoptive parents) of children under the age of six, or of disabled children under the age of 18, and who wish to spend more time with those children, have the legal right to apply to their employers for a more flexible pattern of working hours or (where appropriate) the opportunity to work from home. Although the parents of young children have no legal right to demand more flexible working, their employers are duty-bound both to consider seriously any application for flexible working and to explain their reasons if they feel that they are unable to accommodate the employee's desired work pattern. (*Sources:* ERA 1996, ss.80F-80I; and the **Flexible Working (Procedural Requirements) Regulations 2002**.)

freedom of assembly and association
"Everyone has the right to freedom of peaceful assembly and to freedom of association with

others, including the right to form and to join trade unions for the protection of his interests. No restriction shall be placed on the exercise of these rights other than such as are prescribed by law and are necessary in a democratic society in the interests of national security or public safety, for the prevention of disorder or crime, for the protection of health or morals or for the protection of the rights and freedoms of others." (*Source:* European Convention on Human Rights, Article 11; **Human Rights Act 1998**, Schedule 1.) See also *European Convention on Human Rights* and *Human Rights Act 1998*.

freedom of expression

"Everyone has the right to freedom of expression. This right shall include freedom to hold opinions and to receive and impart information and ideas without interference by public authority and regardless of frontiers...The exercise of these freedoms, since it carries with it duties and responsibilities, may be subject to such formalities, conditions, restrictions or penalties as are prescribed by law and are necessary in a democratic society, in the interests of national security, territorial integrity or public safety, for the prevention of disorder or crime, for the protection of health or morals, for the protection of the reputation or rights of others, for preventing the disclosure of information received in confidence, or for maintaining the authority and impartiality of the judiciary." (*Source:* European Convention on Human Rights, Article 11; **Human Rights Act 1998**, Schedule 1). See also *European Convention on Human Rights* and *Human Rights Act 1998*.

frustration of contract

The common law doctrines of discharge by frustration and supervening impossibility of performance. A contract of employment is said to have been frustrated when one of the parties, usually the employee, is unable to comply with his or her contractual obligations — either through death, a prolonged or permanent illness or disability, or a sentence of imprisonment. The winding-up of a company, the appointment of a receiver, or the dissolution of a partnership will result in most, but not all, cases in the automatic termination of the contracts of employment of the affected employees. In theory at least, the employer is under no obligation to terminate the contract formally or give notice to such an employee that he or she is no longer employed. In practice, given the emergence of unfair dismissal legislation, not to mention the strictures imposed by the **Disability Discrimination Act 1995**, it would be an unwise employer indeed who would rely on the doctrine of frustration to terminate the contract of a long-term sick or absentee employee, without first investigating the circumstances and discussing the matter with the employee.

full-time worker

See *comparable full-time worker*. See also *part-time worker*.

G

gender reassignment

A process which is undertaken under medical supervision for the purpose of reassigning a person's sex by changing physiological or other characteristics of sex, and includes any part of such a process. In the context of employment, it is unlawful for an employer to refuse to offer employment to a person (or to treat that person less favourably than other persons) because he or she intends to undergo, is undergoing or has undergone gender reassignment.

This is the case unless the holder of the job is liable to be called upon to perform intimate physical searches pursuant to statutory powers. The employer could also refuse to offer employment if the nature or location of the establishment makes it impracticable for the holder of the job to live elsewhere than in premises provided by the employer and the premises are inadequate for the purposes of preserving decency and privacy, to the holder of the job sharing accommodation and facilities with either sex while undergoing gender reassignment, and it is not reasonable to expect the employer either to equip those premises with suitable accommodation or to make alternative arrangements. The final situation in which employment could be refused would be if the holder of the job provided vulnerable individuals with personal services promoting their welfare, or similar personal services and, in the reasonable view of the employer, those services could not be effectively provided by a person while that person was undergoing gender reassignment. (*Source:* SDA 1975, ss.7A, 7B and 82.)

genuine occupational qualification

The **Sex Discrimination Act 1975** allows that it is not unlawful to discriminate against a man or a woman by refusing (or deliberately omitting) to offer him or her employment if being a man or a woman is a "genuine occupational qualification" for the job in question. Being a man or a woman is a genuine occupational qualification for a job only where:

- the essential nature of the job calls for a man or a woman for reasons of physiology (excluding physical strength or stamina) or, in dramatic performances or other entertainment, for reasons of authenticity, so that the essential nature of the job would be materially different if carried out by a woman or a man
- the job needs to be held by a man or woman to preserve decency or privacy, because it is likely to involve physical contact with men or

women in circumstances where they might reasonably object to its being carried out by a woman or a man
- the holder of the job is likely to do his or her work in circumstances where men or women might reasonably object to the presence of a man or woman because they are in a state of undress or are using sanitary facilities
- the job is one of two to be held by a married couple
- the job needs to be held by a man because it is likely to involve the performance of duties outside the UK in a country whose laws or customs are such that the duties could not, or could not effectively, be performed by a woman
- the nature or location of the establishment makes it impracticable for the holder of the job to live elsewhere than in premises provided by the employer, and the only such premises which are available for persons holding that kind of job are lived in, or normally lived in, by men (or women) and are not equipped with separate sleeping accommodation for women (or men) or sanitary facilities which could be used by women (or men) in privacy, and it is not reasonable to expect the employer either to equip those premises with such accommodation and facilities or to provide other premises for women (or men).

The "genuine occupational qualification" exception also applies (in prescribed circumstances) to jobs involving work in care homes, prisons, hospitals, the provision of personal services, and work in a private home involving a degree of physical or social contact. (*Source:* SDA 1975, s.7.) See also *direct discrimination, gender reassignment, indirect discrimination, sex discrimination* and *sexual harassment.*

gratuities Tips, gratuities or service charges paid to a worker count towards the national minimum wage (NMW) if, but only if, they are put through the payroll. It follows that tips or gratuities paid directly to workers (eg by customers in restaurants or by hotel guests) do not count towards the national minimum wage, even if such tips, etc are collected and then redistributed to staff by a so-called "troncmaster" (even if the employer is the troncmaster). If they are not put through the payroll, they do not count towards the NMW. (*Source:* **National Minimum Wage Regulations 1999**, regulation 31(1)(e).)

grievances and procedure The written statement of employment particulars, necessarily issued to every employee, must include a note specifying (by description or otherwise) a person to whom the employee can apply for the purpose of seeking redress of any grievance relating to his or her employment, and the manner in which any such application should be made; and, where there are further steps consequent on any such application, explaining those steps or referring to the provisions of a document explaining them which is reasonably accessible to the employee. (*Source:* ERA 1996, ss.1 and 3.) Practical guidance on the development of grievance procedures is to be found in s.2 of ACAS Code of Practice 1 on *Disciplinary and Grievance Procedures*.

gross misconduct Employees are guilty of gross misconduct (warranting summary dismissal) if they act in such a manner as to indicate that they no longer consider themselves bound by, or do not intend to comply with, their obligations under their employment contract (*Freeth v Burr* (1874), LR 9. "Workers should be made aware of the likely consequences of breaking disciplinary rules or failing to meet performance standards. In particular, they should be given a clear indication of the type of conduct, often referred to as gross misconduct, which may warrant summary dismissal (ie dismissal without notice)." (ACAS Code of Practice 1: *Disciplinary and Grievance Procedures*, paragraph 7.)

guarantee payment Employees are entitled to a "guarantee payment" in respect of a workless day if they are not provided with work throughout a day (or shift) during any part of which they are normally required to work in accordance with a contract of employment. This rule applies if the lack of work is due to a diminution in the requirements of the employer's business for work of the kind which the employee is required to do, or any other occurrence affecting the normal working of the employer's business in relation to work of the kind which the employee is employed to do.

However, it does not apply if the employer's inability to provide the employee with work on that day occurs in consequence of a strike, lock-out or other industrial action involving any of its own employees or those employed by an associated employer. To qualify for a guarantee payment in such circumstances, the employees must have been continuously employed for one month or more by the end of the day immediately preceding the relevant workless day; must not unreasonably refuse their employer's offer of suitable alternative work for the day in question (even if that work is not of a kind that the employees are normally employed to do); and must agree to remain "on standby" if asked to do so by their employer. The current (2003/04) guarantee payment is £17.30 a day or the employee's normal wages in respect of that day (whichever is the lesser of those amounts) payable for each of a maximum of five workless days in any period of three consecutive months. (*Source:* ERA 1996, ss.28-35.)

H

harassment, alarm and distress

The term "harassment" includes words or conduct calculated to cause alarm or distress to the victim of such conduct. It is a criminal offence for any person (whether in the course of employment or otherwise) to pursue a course of conduct that amounts to the harassment of another person and that the harasser knows (or ought to know) amounts to such harassment. A person guilty of such an offence is liable, on summary conviction, to a fine of up to £5000 and/or imprisonment for a term not exceeding six months. Furthermore, the victim of such harassment may pursue a claim for damages in the ordinary courts and may apply for a High Court or county court injunction restraining the defendant from any further conduct amounting to harassment. Failure to comply with that order is again an offence, for which the penalty on conviction is an unlimited fine and/or imprisonment for up to five years. (*Source:* **Protection from Harassment Act 1997**, ss.1, 2 and 3.)

A person is likewise guilty of an offence and liable to a fine of up to £5000 (and/or imprisonment for up to six months) "if, with intent to cause a person, harassment, alarm or distress, he or she uses threatening, abusive or insulting words or behaviour, or disorderly behaviour, or displays any writing, sign or other visible representation which is threatening, abusive or insulting, thereby causing that other person harassment, alarm or distress". (*Source:* **Public Order Act 1986**, s.4A.) See also *sexual harassment*.

health and capabilities assessment

Employers are required to offer young workers undertaking night work a health and capabilities assessment. Under the **Working Time Regulations 1998** an employer must not assign a young worker to work during the period between 10.00pm and 6.00am (the "restricted period") unless the employer has ensured that the young worker will have the opportunity of a free assessment of his or her health and capabilities before taking up the assignment; or the young worker had an assessment of his or her health and capabilities before being assigned to work during the restricted period on an earlier occasion and the employer has no reason to believe that that assessment is no longer valid. The employer shall further ensure that young workers employed by it and assigned to work during the restricted period have the opportunity of free assessments of their health and capabilities at regular intervals of whatever duration may be appropriate. Should a registered medical practitioner advise an employer that a night worker is suffering from health problems associated with night work, and it is possible to transfer the worker to suitable alternative day work, the employer must transfer the worker accordingly. (*Source:* WTR 1998, regulation 7(2) and (6).) See also *health assessment*.

Health and Safety at Work, etc Act 1974

Section 2 of the 1974 Act states that it shall be the duty of every employer to ensure, so far as is reasonably practicable, the health, safety and welfare at work of all his or her employees. The matters to which that duty extends include, in particular:

- the provision of plant and systems of work that are...safe and without risks to health; arrangements for ensuring...safety and absence of risks to health in connection with the use, handling, storage and transport of articles and substances

- the provision of such information, instruction, training and supervision as is necessary to ensure... the health and safety at work of his employees
- the maintenance of any place of work under the employer's control... in a condition that is safe and without risks to health and the provision and maintenance of means of access to and egress from it that are safe and without such risks
- and the provision and maintenance of a safe working environment for his employees that is... safe, without risks to health, and adequate as regards facilities and arrangements for their welfare at work.

An employer (including any director, manager or other similar officer of the body corporate) who fails to comply with its primary duties under the 1974 Act is guilty of an offence and liable, on summary conviction, to a fine of up to £20,000 (for each offence) or, if convicted on indictment, a fine of an unlimited amount. (*Source:* HASAWA 1974, ss.2, 33 and 37.)

health assessment An adult worker (ie a worker who has attained the age of 18) must not be assigned to night work without first being afforded an opportunity of a free health assessment, unless he or she had a health assessment before being assigned to such work on an earlier occasion and the employer has no reason to believe that that earlier assessment is no longer valid. An employer should also see to it that every adult night worker is offered the opportunity of repeat health assessments at regular intervals. Should a registered medical practitioner advise an employer that a night worker is suffering from health problems associated with night work, and it is possible to transfer the worker to suitable alternative day work, the employer must transfer the worker accordingly. (*Source:* WTR 1998, regulation 7(1) and (6).) See also *health and capabilities assessment* and *young worker*.

holidays, annual

See *annual holidays*.

home worker

An individual who contracts with a person for the purposes of that person's business, for the execution of work to be done in a place not under the control or management of that person. In determining for the purposes of the **National Minimum Wage Act 1998** whether a home worker is or is not a worker, the definition of worker in that Act shall have effect as if for the word "personally" in that definition there were substituted the words: "whether personally or otherwise". (*Source:* NMWA 1998, s.35.)

hours of work: workers aged 18 and over

Under the **Working Time Regulations 1998** (as amended), every worker aged 18 and over (other than in an adult worker working in an excepted or excluded occupation) has the right not to be required to work more than an average of 48 hours a week (including overtime hours) calculated over a reference period of 17 consecutive weeks. An adult night worker has the right not to be required to work more than an average of eight hours in any 24-hour period calculated over that same reference period. The averaging period may be extended in certain circumstances. A worker may agree to work more than an average of 48 hours a week so long as he or she does so individually, voluntarily and in writing. If the opt-out agreement (which must be signed personally by the worker) does not remind the worker of his or her right to cancel the agreement on giving a specified period of notice (not exceeding three months), the worker may cancel that agreement on giving seven days' notice. Any term in a collective or workforce agreement that purports to override an individual's right to opt-out of the maximum 48-hour week is void and unenforceable. A worker who is victimised, disciplined or subjected to any other detriment (including termination of employment) for asserting his or her rights under the 1998 Regulations may complain to an employment tribunal and will be awarded substantial compensation if that complaint is upheld. (*Sources:* ERA 1996, ss.45A, 101A and 104; WTR 1998, Part II). See also *hours of work: workers under the age of 18, annual holidays, rest breaks* and *rest periods (daily and weekly)*.

hours of work: workers under the age of 18

From 6 April 2003, no young worker under the age of 18 may lawfully be employed for more than eight hours a day or for more than 48 hours a week (a week for these purposes being the period of seven consecutive days that begins on a Sunday and ends at midnight on the following Saturday). However, these restrictions do not apply if, but only if, each of the following circumstances applies:

(a) the work needs to be done either to maintain continuity of service or production or in response to a surge in demand for a service or product

(b) there is no adult worker available to perform the work, and

(c) performing the work would not adversely affect the young worker's education or training.

Furthermore, no young worker under the age of 18 may lawfully be employed during the "restricted period" that is to say, during the period between 10.00pm and 6.00am (or, if a young worker's contract provides for him or her to work after 10.00pm, the period between 11.00pm and 7.00am). However, this restriction does not apply to young workers employed in hospitals or similar establishment, or in connection with cultural, artistic or advertising activities where each of the circumstances described in (a), (b) and (c) apply; nor (save for an absolute prohibition on employment between midnight and 4.00am) does it apply to workers employed in agriculture, retail trading, hotels, bakeries, catering establishments (including restaurants and bars), or in postal or newspaper deliveries if, but only if, each of the circumstances described in (a), (b) and (c) apply. The reader will note that the restrictions on the working hours of young persons are absolute. There is no provision for averaging working time over a reference period; nor can individuals opt out of those restrictions. (*Source:* **Working Time Regulations 1998**, regulations 4A, 5A and 27A, as inserted by the **Working Time (Amendment) Regulations 2002**.) See also *annual holidays, health and capabilities assessment, rest breaks* and *rest periods (daily and weekly)*.

Human Rights Act 1998

An Act to give "further effect" to the rights and freedoms guaranteed to all citizens under the European Convention on Human Rights. The 1998 Act, which came into force in the UK on 2 October 2000, does not create any new statutory or common law rights. What it does do is impose a duty on "public authorities" (government departments, local authorities, borough councils, the police, health authorities and the like) to act in a way that is compatible with a Convention right. It likewise imposes a duty on the tribunals and courts (as public authorities in their own right), when determining a question which has arisen in connection with a Convention right, to take into account any relevant judgment, decision, declaration or advisory opinion of the European Court of Human Rights (ECHR); any opinion or decision of the European Commission of Human Rights; and any decision of the

Committee of Ministers under Article 46 (as to the jurisdiction of the ECHR). Furthermore, without affecting their validity, continuing operation or enforcement, UK primary and subordinate legislation (eg statutes, regulations and orders) must be read and given effect in a way that is compatible with the Convention rights. (*Source:* HRA 1998, s.3.)

I

illegal immigrant

A foreign national subject to immigration control who does not have the valid and subsisting right to enter or remain in the UK, or who is subject to a condition precluding him or her from taking up employment while in the UK. Any person who employs an illegal immigrant aged 16 and over is guilty of an offence and liable on summary conviction to a fine of up to £5000. (*Source:* **Asylum and Immigration Act 1996**, s.8.)

immunity, trade union

The immunity from actions in tort enjoyed by the trade unions before 1971 and, to a lesser extent, between 1971 and 1974, has now been largely eroded. The current position is outlined in Part V of the **Trade Union and Labour Relations (Consolidation) Act 1992**. The immunity of a trade union from actions in tort arising out of strikes or other industrial action only applies to official action (ie action supported by a properly-conducted ballot) taken in contemplation or furtherance of a trade dispute. There is no immunity if the principal executive committee of a trade union does not act speedily to repudiate unofficial industrial action by its members; or if the union engages in secondary action which is not lawful picketing. Industrial action is also excluded from protection if designed to put pressure on an employer not to employ (or continue employing) persons who are not members of a trade union, or to impose a union membership agreement (ie a closed shop); or if done by way of protest against the dismissal of one or more employees dismissed for taking part in unofficial industrial action.

implied term

A term in a contract of employment that is not specifically set out or stated in the contract itself. Employers have an implied contractual duty not to act in a way calculated (or likely) to destroy, or seriously damage, the relationship of trust and confidence which should exist between them and their employees (eg by verbally abusing or sexually harassing an employee, imposing a unilateral cut in pay, transferring an employee to another location in the absence of any contractual right to do so; and so on). Employers also have a common law and implied contractual duty to take reasonable care for the health and safety of the workers in their employ. For their part, employees have an implied contractual obligation to carry out their duties diligently, efficiently and safely; to obey their employers' reasonable instructions; and not to do anything calculated to undermine their employers' reputation (eg by disclosing their employers' trade secrets, marketing strategies, pricing policies and other confidential information to unauthorised third parties). A breach of an implied term could lead to the dismissal of the offending party, claims for damages and restraint orders, or (if the employer is the offending party) claims for damages and/or complaints of unfair constructive dismissal. See also *care, duty of, constructive dismissal* and *express terms.*

inadmissible reasons for dismissal

An employee (or other worker), dismissed on grounds of sex, race, disability or trade union membership (or non-membership), or for having made a protected disclosure, or for having asserted (or taken advantage of) his or her statutory employment rights, or for questioning or challenging any alleged infringement of those rights, may complain to an employment tribunal regardless of his or her age or length of service at the material time. In short, such a dismissal is *prima facie* inadmissible and automatically unfair. (*Sources:* TULRA 1992, ERA 1996, SDA 1975, RRA 1976, DDA 1995.)

incapacity for work An employee who is incapacitated (or deemed to be incapacitated) for work, through illness or injury, for more than four calendar days, is entitled, subject to certain qualifying conditions, to be paid statutory sick pay (SSP) by his or her employer for up to 28 weeks in any single period, or series of linked periods, of incapacity for work. (*Source:* **Statutory Sick Pay (General) Regulations 1982** (as amended).) Lack of capability assessed by reference (amongst other things) to an employee's health or any other physical or mental quality is one of the five so-called permitted reasons for dismissal. (*Source:* ERA 1996, ss.98(2)(a) and (3).

independent trade union A trade union is deemed an independent trade union (certified as such by the Certification Officer) if it is not under the domination or control of an employer or a group of employers or of one or more employers' associations, and is not liable to interference by an employer or any such group or association (arising out of the provision of financial or material support or by any other means whatever) tending towards such control. (*Source:* ERA 1996, s.235.)

indirect discrimination Sections 1(2) and (4) of the **Sex Discrimination Act 1975** (SDA) state that an employer is guilty of unlawful indirect discrimination against a woman if "on the grounds of her sex, he treats her less favourably than he treats or would treat a man, or he applies to her a provision, criterion or practice which he applies or would apply equally to a man, but which is such that it would be to the detriment of a considerably larger proportion of women than of men, and which he cannot show to be justifiable irrespective of the sex of the person to whom it is applied, and which is to her detriment. If an employer treats or would treat a man differently according to the man's marital status, his treatment of a woman is to be compared to his treatment of a man having the like marital status." Sections 1(2) and (4) are to be read as applying equally to men, save that "no account shall be taken of special treatment afforded to women in connection with pregnancy or childbirth" (SDA, s.2).

Similar provisions are to be found in the **Race Relations Act 1976** which states (at s.1(1)(b)) that a person (eg an employer) discriminates against another on racial grounds if "he applies to that person a requirement or condition which he applies or would apply equally to persons not of the same racial group as that other but which is such that the proportion of persons of the same racial group who can comply with it is considerably smaller than the proportion of persons not of that racial group who can comply with it, and which he cannot show to be justifiable irrespective of the colour, race, nationality or ethnic or national origins of the person to who it is applied; and which is to the detriment of that other because he cannot comply with it". There is no upper limit on the amount of compensation that may be awarded by the employment tribunals when complaints of unlawful sex or racial discrimination (direct or indirect) are upheld.

industrial action   A concerted stoppage of work or any other form of industrial action short of a strike (eg an overtime or call-out ban), whether or not it involves a breach or interference with an employee's contract of employment. Employees who take part in unofficial industrial action (ie action that is not in furtherance of a genuine trade dispute and has not received majority support through a properly conduct secret ballot) have no immunity from dismissal and no right to complain of unfair dismissal, unless the action in question is speedily repudiated in writing by a responsible officer of the relevant union's national executive committee and the employee returns to work by the end of the working day following the day on which that repudiation was notified. An employee who takes part in official industrial action may likewise be dismissed with impunity if he or she is still on strike eight weeks after the strike began, in spite of all genuine efforts by the parties to resolve the dispute by conciliation. Immunity from dismissal will also be forfeit if an employer dismisses all of the employees taking part in official industrial action and does not re-engage any of those employees within the next three months.

For further information, the reader is commended to DTI booklets PL 869 (*Industrial action and the law*) and PL 870 (*Industrial action and the law: a guide for employers, their customers and suppliers and others*), available from the DTI Publications Orderline on 0870 1502 500 or from *publications@dti.gsi.gov.uk*. (*Source:* TULRA 1992, Part V.)

Information Commissioner

Formerly the Data Protection Commissioner, the role of the Information Commissioner is to monitor and promote adherence to the **Data Protection Act 1998** and, after consultations with trade associations and other interested parties and bodies, prepare and disseminate codes of practice containing guidance for employers and others on the processing of personal data. (*Source:* DPA 1998, Part VI.)

insolvency of employers

Under the **Insolvency Act 1986**, certain monies owed to employees when their employers become insolvent or go into receivership are treated as preferential debts (subject to a maximum of £800 in respect of the four-month period immediately preceding the date of the relevant receiving order or the appointment of the provisional liquidator). Amounts in excess of £800 (or in respect of longer periods) are treated as ordinary debts. Given that employees may have to wait a considerable time to recover monies (including preferential debts) owed to them by their insolvent employers (with no guarantee of success), the **Employment Rights Act 1996** empowers the Secretary of State to pay debts owed to such employees from the National Insurance Fund (NI Fund) and to assume the role of preferred or ordinary creditor in their place. However, there are limits on the amounts payable from the NI Fund in these circumstances and the debts to which they relate. To summarise, the Secretary of State (once satisfied as to the nature and extent of the debts in question) may reimburse arrears of pay (including overtime payments, commission, statutory guarantee payments, statutory sick pay, etc) for a period not exceeding eight weeks (at a maximum of £260 per week); money in lieu of notice (again subject to a maximum of £260 per week); a maximum of six weeks' holiday pay in respect of the period of 12 months preceding the employer's solvency (at a maximum of £260 per week); and the amount of any basic award of compensation for unfair dismissal. (*Sources:* **Insolvency Act 1986**, s.386, Schedule 6; ERA 1996, Part XII.)

instant dismissal

See *summary dismissal*.

insurance, compulsory

Every employer is duty-bound to insure (and maintain insurance) "against liability for bodily injury or disease sustained by his employees and arising out of and in the course of their employment". The insurance cover (for a minimum of £5 million) must be effected with an authorised insurer. The Certificate of Employer's Liability Insurance must be kept available for inspection by the relevant enforcing authority (ie a Health and Safety Executive (HSE) or local authority inspectors) while a copy (or copies) of that Certificate must be displayed in the employer's premises in a position (or positions) where it can be easily seen and read by every employee. A failure to comply with these requirements is a criminal offence for which the penalty on summary conviction is a fine of up to £2500 and a further fine of £2500 a day for each day of continued non-compliance. (*Source:* **Employers' Liability (Compulsory Insurance) Act 1969.**) See also *care, duty of.*

interim relief

A tribunal order for interim relief is an order for the reinstatement or re-engagement of a dismissed employee or for the continued payment of the employee's wages or salary pending a full tribunal hearing concerning the fairness or otherwise of the employee's dismissal. Applications for interim relief must normally be submitted to an employment tribunal within seven days of the effective date of termination of the employee's contract of employment. Such an application, which must be heard as soon as practicable, will be accepted if an employment tribunal is satisfied that there is *prima facie* evidence that the employee was dismissed for carrying out (or presuming to carry out) his or her functions as a trade union-appointed safety representative, a representative of employee safety, a member of a safety committee, a competent person (designated as such in accordance with regulation 7 of the **Management of Health and Safety at Work**

Regulations 1999), a workforce representative, a trustee of a relevant occupational pension scheme, an employee representative; for having made a protected disclosure; or for supporting or not supporting an application for recognition by an independent trade union. (*Source:* ERA 1996, ss.128-132.)

inventions, ownership of

In law, an invention made by an employee will be taken to belong to his or her employer:

(a) if it was made in the course of the employee's normal duties in circumstances such that an invention might reasonably be expected to result from the carrying out of those duties, or

(b) if it was made in the course of the duties of the employee and the nature of those duties and the employee's particular responsibilities were such that he had a special obligation to further the interests of his employer's undertaking.

However, once the employer has applied for and been granted a patent, the employee may apply to the Comptroller-General of Patents, Designs and Patents (or, if need be, to the High Court or Court of Session) for an award of compensation, ie a fair share of the benefit that the employer has derived (or might reasonably expect to derive) from the patent. Any term in a contract of employment that purports to diminish an employee's statutory rights in this regard is void and unenforceable. (*Source:* **Patents Act 1977**, ss.39-43.) See also *copyright ownership*.

itemised pay statement

"An employee has the right to be given by his employer, at or before the time at which any payment of wages or salary is made to him, a written itemised pay statement". An itemised pay statement must specify:

(a) the gross amount of the wages or salary

payable to the employee in respect of the pay period in question

(b) the amount of any fixed deductions and the purposes for which they are made

(c) the amount and purpose of each and every variable deduction (eg PAYE tax, National Insurance Contributions, tax credits, etc); and

(d) the net amount of the wages or salary payable to the employee on that occasion."

If there are a great many fixed deductions, the employer may aggregate those deductions on the employee's pay slip so long as the employee has already been provided with a so-called standing statement of fixed deductions, which must be amended and reissued as and when required or at least once every twelve months. An employer who refuses or fails to provide an employee with an itemised pay statement (or with a statement that complies with the above requirements) will be ordered by an employment tribunal to repay to the employee all unnotified and undeclared deductions (even if the employee had previously agreed to those deductions). (*Source:* ERA 1996, ss.8-12.)

J

job

In relation to an employee, "job" means the nature of the work which the employee is employed to do in accordance with his or her contract of employment and the capacity and place in which he or she is so employed. The written statement of employment particulars, necessarily issued to every employee (within two months of the date on which he or she starts work) must include particulars of "the title of the job which the employee is employed to do or a brief description of the work for which he is employed". (*Source:* ERA 1996, ss.1 and 235.)

job description   A document containing a description of the work an employee is employed to do (including, advisedly, an assessment of any health and safety risks associated with that job). Although employers are under no strict legal obligation to provide their employees with detailed job descriptions, the written statement of employment particulars, necessarily issued to every new employee (within two months of the date on which he or she starts work) must include particulars (amongst other things) of "the title of the job which the employee is employed to do or a brief description of the work for which he or she is employed". Should a question arise before an employment tribunal concerning the precise nature and extent of an employee's contractual duties (eg the existence of a mobility clause), the employee's job description (if such exists) would be admissible in evidence in any such proceedings. (*Source:* ERA 1996, ss.1 and 235.)

job title   See *job.*

L

lay-offs and short-time working   Employees whose remuneration under their contract is dependent on their being provided with work, will be taken to be laid off for a week if they are not provided with work of the kind they are employed to do throughout that week and receive no payment in respect of that week. Employees, on the other hand, will be taken to be kept on short time for a week if, by reason of a diminution in the work provided by their employer (being work of a kind which they are employed to do), the employee's remuneration for the week is less than half a week's pay. Employees who are laid off or kept on short-time working for four or more consecutive weeks (or for six or more weeks in the aggregate within a period of 13 consecutive weeks) are entitled in prescribed circumstances to serve notice on their employer to terminate their contract and lay claim to a statutory redundancy payment. It is important to note that, in the absence of any express term to the contrary in the contract of employment, an employer has no common law or implied contractual right to lay off employees or keep them on short-time working. To do otherwise is a breach of contract that could give rise to a claim for damages arising out of that breach and/or a complaint of unfair constructive dismissal. (*Source:* ERA 1996 ss.147-154.) See also *guarantee payment*.

less favourable treatment, written reasons for

Fixed-term employees (or part-time workers) who believe that they are being, or have been, treated less favourably than comparable permanent employees (or comparable full-time workers) in the same establishment may write to their employers demanding a written explanation for that less favourable treatment. An employer must provide that explanation within the next 21 days. A refusal or failure to do so is admissible as evidence in proceedings before an employment tribunal. It is as well to note that employees and other workers have no need to resign or quit their jobs in order to bring such proceedings. Indeed, if they are dismissed, selected for redundancy, or subjected to any other detriment for asserting their statutory rights in this way, or for questioning or challenging any alleged infringement of their statutory rights, whether before an employment tribunal or otherwise, they may complain (or complain again) to an employment tribunal (regardless of their ages or length of service at the material time) and will be awarded substantial compensation if their complaints are upheld. (*Sources:* PTWR 2000; FTER 2002.) See also *fixed-term employee* and *part-time worker*.

like work　　　Within the context of the **Equal Pay Act 1970**, a woman is to be regarded as employed on like work with men in the same employment if, but only if, her work and theirs is of the same or of a broadly similar nature, and the differences (if any) between the things she does and the things they do are not of practical importance in relation to terms and conditions of employment; and, accordingly, in comparing her work with theirs, regard shall be had to the frequency or otherwise with which any such differences occur in practice as well as to the nature and extent of the differences. (*Source:* EqPA 1970, ss.1(2)(a) and (4).) See also *equal pay*.

limited-term contract　　　A contract of employment is a "limited-term contract" if the employee's employment under that contract is not intended to be permanent, and provision is accordingly made in the contract for it to terminate by virtue of a limiting event (*Source:* ERA 1996, s.235(2A).)

limiting event　　　A "limiting event", in relation to a contract of employment, means:

(a) in the case of a contract for a fixed term, the expiry of the term

(b) in the case of a contract made in contemplation of the performance of a specific task, the performance of the task, and

(c) in the case of a contract which provides for its termination on the occurrence of an event (or the failure of an event to occur) the occurrence of the event (or the failure of the event to occur).

(*Source:* ERA 1996, s.235(2B).) See also *dismissal, meaning of, fixed-term employee* and *limited-term contract*.

live-in accommodation　　　An employer who provides live-in accommodation for any worker (such as a hotel worker) may offset part (but not all) of the rent charged for that accommodation against the national minimum wage (NMW) payable to that worker in respect of the relevant pay reference period. The most that an employer may offset against the NMW by way of accommodation charges is 57p per hour, for each of a worker's contractual working hours — or £22.75 a week — whichever is the lower of those amounts. It follows that, if a worker is contracted to work a 35-hour week, the maximum amount of rent that may be offset against his or her NMW is £19.85 a week. If a worker occupies live-in accommodation for less than a whole week (eg five days), the maximum daily amount that may be offset against the NMW is 57p per hour for each of the worker's contractual (or average) daily working hours, subject to a maximum of £3.25 a day. A "day" for these purposes is the period from midnight to midnight. (*Source:* NMWR 1999, regulations 30(d), 31(1) (i), 36 and 37.)

look for work, time off to

Employees under notice of redundancy have the legal right to be permitted a reasonable amount of paid time off work to look for employment elsewhere (attend interviews, etc) and/or make arrangements for re-training. However, they will not qualify for that right unless they will have been (or would have been) continuously employed for a period of two years or more by the date on which their redundancy notice is due to expire; or, if no notice was give, by the date on which it would expire were it the statutory minimum period of notice prescribed by s.86 of the **Employment Rights Act 1996**. An employer who refuses to permit paid time off in these circumstances will be ordered by an employment tribunal to pay the employee the equivalent of two days' pay. (*Source:* ERA 1996, ss.52-54.)

M

manual records   See *relevant filing system.*

marital status   See *sex discrimination.*

maternity grounds,   See *suspension on maternity grounds.*
suspension on

maternity leave,   An employee who exercises her right to ordinary
rights during   maternity leave is entitled to the benefit of the
terms and conditions of employment which
would have applied to her but for her absence
from work (save for her right to be paid her
normal wages or salary during her absence).
Furthermore, she remains bound by any
obligations arising under those terms and
conditions, and is entitled to return from leave to
the job in which she was employed before her
absence began. (*Source:* ERA 1996, s.71.) See also
statutory maternity pay.

An employee who exercises her right to
additional maternity leave is entitled, during her
absence, to the benefit of her employer's implied
obligation to her of trust and confidence and any
terms and conditions of her employment relating
to notice of termination, compensation in the
event of redundancy, or disciplinary or grievance
procedures. For her part, she remains bound
during her absence to her implied obligation to
her employer of good faith and by any terms and
conditions of her employment relating to notice
to terminate her contract, the disclosure of
confidential information, the acceptance of gifts
or other benefits, or her participation in any other
business. Other than in prescribed circumstances,
she has the right to return to work in the job in
which she was employed before her ordinary
maternity leave period began. (*Sources:* ERA
1996, s.73; **Maternity and Parental Leave, etc
Regulations 1999**, regulation 17.)

maternity pay   See *statutory maternity pay.*

maternity pay period   The period during which statutory maternity pay (SMP) is payable to an employee absent from work on ordinary maternity leave. For an employee whose expected week of childbirth (EWC) began before 6 April 2003, the first week of the maternity pay period is the week that begins on the Sunday of the week immediately following the week in which she left work to begin her maternity leave (a "week" for these purposes being the period of seven consecutive days that begins on a Sunday). If she returns to work with the same (or another) employer after her baby is born, but before the end of her ordinary maternity leave, her maternity pay period ends on the Saturday of the week immediately preceding the week in which she returned to work with her original employer (or started work with that other employer). (*Source:* **Statutory Maternity Pay (General) Regulations 1986.**)

The maternity pay period for an employee, whose EWC begins on or after 6 April 2003, is the period of up to 26 weeks beginning on the day immediately following the day on which she started her maternity leave (a week for these purposes being the seven-day period starting with the day in question and each subsequent seven-day period starting on that same day of the week). If she returns to work with the same (or another) employer after giving birth before the end of her ordinary maternity leave, her maternity pay period ends with the last payment week before the week in which she returned to work (or started work with that other employer). (*Source:* **Statutory Maternity Pay (General) Regulations 1986**, as amended by the **Social**

Security, Statutory Maternity Pay and Statutory Sick Pay (Miscellaneous Amendments) Regulations 2002.)

maternity rights   Every pregnant employee has the legal right to take up to 18 weeks' ordinary maternity leave (26 weeks, if her expected week of childbirth (EWC) begins on or after 6 April 2003), followed (if she qualifies) by a period of up to 29 weeks' additional maternity leave (calculated from the beginning of the week in which childbirth occurred) or, if her EWC begins on or after 6 April, by a period of up to 26 weeks' additional maternity leave (beginning on the day immediately following the day on which her ordinary maternity leave period ends). Unless she gives birth prematurely, an employee may not begin her ordinary maternity leave earlier than the beginning of the 11th week before her EWC. An employee on maternity leave has the right to return to work in the job in which she was employed before her absence began or (in specified circumstances) a suitable alternative job. An employee with average weekly earnings equal to, or greater than, the current lower earnings limit for NI contributions, will qualify for statutory maternity pay (SMP) during her ordinary maternity leave period. (*Sources:* ERA 1996, Part VIII, Chapter I; the **Maternity and Parental Leave, etc Regulations 1999**, the **Maternity and Parental Leave (Amendment) Regulations 2002; Social Security, Statutory Maternity Pay and Statutory Sick Pay (Miscellaneous Amendments) Regulations 2002.**)

medical grounds, suspension on   See *suspension on medical grounds.*

medical report   In the case of an individual, means a report relating to the physical or mental health of that individual prepared by a medical practitioner (ie a person registered under the **Medical Act 1983**) who is or has been responsible for the clinical care of the individual. Under the **Access to Medical Reports Act 1988**, an employer or other person may not apply to a medical practitioner for a medical report relating to any employee (or would-be employee), for employment or insurance purposes, unless the employee in question has been notified of the employer's intentions and has consented to the making of that application (eg by countersigning a clause to that effect in the employer's application or by signing a separate consent form). Employees must also be informed of their rights under the 1998 Act, including their right to intercept the medical report before it is supplied and to ask the doctor to amend any part of the report which they consider to be incorrect or misleading. If the doctor is not prepared to make the suggested amendments or corrections, the employee or candidate may attach a statement to the report containing his or her views in respect of any part of the report that the doctor has declined to amend.

mobility clause

An express (or, more difficult to prove, an implied) term in an employee's contract of employment giving the employer the right, on reasonable notice, to transfer or relocate the employee to another location or establishment within the employer's business or organisation. The written statement of employment particulars necessarily issued to all new employees (within two months of the date on which each of those employees starts work) must specify either the employee's place of work or, where he or she is required or permitted to work at various places, an indication of that and of the employer's address. In the absence of any such express or implied term in an employee's contract of employment, an employer who, regardless, transfers the employee to another location is in breach of contract which could prompt the employee to resign (with or without notice) and pursue a complaint of unfair constructive dismissal before an employment tribunal. (*Source:* ERA 1996. ss.1 and 95(1)(c).)

N

national minimum wage

Every worker in the UK, who has attained the age of 18, must be paid the appropriate national minimum wage (NMW). From 1 October 2002, the NMW for workers aged 22 and over is £4.20 per hour; and for workers aged 18 to 21, inclusive, £3.60 per hour. The NMW for workers aged 22 and over, who are in receipt of accredited training for 26 days or more during their first six months of employment, is likewise £3.60 per hour. The term "accredited training" means training undertaken with a new employer during normal working hours (at or away from the workplace) which leads to a vocational qualification approved by the Secretary of State for Education and Skills. It does not apply to in-house training (such as induction or on-the-job training) devised and provided by employers. There is presently no NMW for workers under the age of 18. Certain payments and benefits (such as overtime premium payments, shift allowances, unsociable hours payments, tips, gratuities, etc) do not count towards the NMW. An employer who refuses or fails to pay the appropriate NMW to any worker is guilty of an offence and liable, on summary conviction, to a fine of up to £5000, for each offence. Employers must keep adequate records and must make those records available for inspection (on request) by individual workers and Inland Revenue enforcement officers. Employers needing advice on the NMW may call the Confidential NMW Helpline on 0845 6000 678. (*Sources:* NMWA 1998; **National Minimum Wage Regulations 1999.**)

new or expectant mothers

An employee is a "new or expectant mother" if she is pregnant or breastfeeding or has given birth within the previous six months. If the persons working in a particular undertaking include women of child-bearing age and the work is of a kind that could involve risk, by reason of her condition, to the health and safety of a new or expectant mother (or to that of her baby) from any processes or working conditions, or physical, biological or chemical agents, the employer must, when conducting the risk assessment prescribed by regulation 3(1) of the **Management of Health and Safety at Work Regulations 1999**, identify that risk and take appropriate steps to eliminate or minimise it. If this proves to be impracticable and the risk cannot be avoided by altering the employee's working conditions or hours of work, the employer must suspend the employee from work on full pay for so long as is necessary to avoid the risk. (*Source:* MHSWR 1999, regulation 16.) See also *night work: new or expectant mothers, rest facilities: new and expectant mothers* and *risk assessment.*

night time

In relation to a worker, "night time" means the period of seven or more hours (including the period between midnight and 5.00am) specified as such under the terms of a collective or workforce agreement or, in the absence of any such agreement, the period between 11.00pm and 6.00am. (*Source:* WTR 1998, regulation 2.)

night work

Means work during night time. (*Source:* WTR 1998, regulation 2.)

night work: new or expectant mothers

If a new or expectant mother works at night, and a certificate from a registered medical practitioner or a registered midwife shows that it is necessary for her health or safety that she should not be at work for any period of such work identified in the certificate, her employer must either transfer her to suitable alternative work during the day or suspend her from work on full pay for so long as is necessary for her health and safety. (*Sources:* ERA 1996, s.67; MHSWR 1999, regulation 17.) See also *suspension on maternity grounds.*

night worker

For the purposes of the **Working Time Regulations 1998**, a worker is a "night worker" if, as a normal course, he or she works at least three hours of his daily working time during night time, or if he or she is likely, during night time, to work at least such proportion of his or her annual working time as may be specified in a collective or workforce agreement. A person works at least three hours during night time, as a "normal course", if he or she works such hours on the majority of days on which he or she works. Night workers, whose work involves special hazards or heavy physical or mental strain (identified by the employer's risk assessment, or in a collective or workforce agreement, as posing as significant risk to their health and safety) must not be required to work for more than eight hours in any 24-hour period during which they work at night. (*Source:* WTR 1998, regulations 2 and 6.) See also *health assessment.*

non-discrimination notice

A so-called "non-discrimination notice" may be served by the Equal Opportunities Commission, the Commission for Racial Equality or the Disability Rights Commission on recalcitrant employers (and others) who persist in flouting sex, race or disability discrimination legislation

— requiring them to cease their unlawful practices and to furnish evidence of their compliance with the terms of the notice over the next five years. Should an employer contravene the terms of a non-discrimination notice, the relevant Commission may refer the matter for determination by an employment tribunal and/or apply to a county court (or sheriff court) for an injunction (or order) restraining it from doing so. A failure to comply with such an injunction is a contempt of court which could lead to a substantial fine and/or imprisonment. (*Sources:* SDA 1975, ss.67-70; RRA 1976 ss.58-61; **Disability Rights Commission Act 1999**, ss.4–5 and Schedule 3.) See also *disability discrimination, racial discrimination* and *sex discrimination*.

normal retiring age

To qualify to pursue a complaint of unfair dismissal before an employment tribunal, an employee must (a) have been continuously employed for one year or more and (b) have been under "normal retiring age", at the effective date of termination of his or her contract of employment. The normal retiring age for an employee is the age at which that employee (and any other person occupying the position the employee held) would normally be required to retire in the undertaking in question, so long as that retiring age is the same regardless of the sex of the person holding the position the employee held. If there is no readily-identifiable retiring age for employees occupying the same or similar jobs in the relevant undertaking, that normal retiring age will be held to be 65. It should be noted that qualifying conditions (a) and (b) above do not apply to an employee allegedly dismissed for an inadmissible or unlawful reason. (*Source:* ERA 1996, s.109(1) and (2).)

notice of termination

The written statement of employment particulars necessarily issued to every new employee, within two months of the date on which he or she starts work, must (amongst other things) specify the length of notice which the employee is required to give and entitled to receive to terminate his or her contract of employment. In law, the minimum notice required to be given by an employee who has been continuously employed for one month or more is one week. Save for any contrary term in the employee's contract, that statutory minimum period of notice does not increase with length of service.

The minimum notice an employer is required to give an employee who has been continuously employed for one month or more, but less than two years, is one week and, thereafter, one additional week's notice for each subsequent year of continuous employment, subject to a maximum of 12 weeks' notice on completion of 12 or more years' continuous service. Any term in a contract of employment or related document that purports to undermine an employee's right to minimum notice is void and unenforceable. However, an employee who is summarily dismissed for gross misconduct thereby forfeits his or her right to notice. However, there is nothing to prevent either party to a contract of employment from waiving his or her right to notice on any occasion or from accepting a payment in lieu of notice. (*Source:* ERA 1996, ss.86-91.) See also *pay in lieu of notice.*

O

occupational pension scheme trustees

See *pension scheme trustees* and *time off work: general.*

offenders, rehabilitation of

See *Rehabilitation of Offenders Act 1974.*

ordinary maternity leave

A pregnant employee whose expected week of childbirth (EWC) begins (or began) before 6 April 2003 has the legal right to take up to 18 weeks' ordinary maternity leave. To exercise that right she must notify her employer, at least 21 days before the date in question, of the date on which she intends to start her leave and, if asked to do so, must produce for her employer's inspection a certificate of expected confinement signed by her doctor or registered midwife. However, unless she gives birth prematurely, she may not begin her ordinary maternity leave before the beginning of the 11th week before her EWC. A pregnant employee, whose EWC begins on or after 6 April 2003, has the legal right to take up to 26 weeks' ordinary maternity leave. To exercise that right she must notify her employer, by the end of the 15th week before her EWC, of the date on which she intends to start her leave and, if asked to do so, must produce for her employer's inspection a certificate of expected confinement signed by her doctor or registered midwife. However, unless she gives birth prematurely, she may not begin her ordinary maternity leave before the beginning of the 11th week before her EWC. (*Sources:* ERA 1996, ss.71-75; **Maternity and Parental Leave, etc Regulations 1999**, as amended by the **Maternity and Parental Leave, etc Amendment Regulations 2002**.) See also *additional maternity leave, return to work,* and *maternity rights.*

ordinary adoption leave

See *adoption leave.*

P

paper-based records See *relevant filing system.*

parental leave

The employed parents of a child who is under the age of five (or 18, if adopted) have the legal right to take up to 13 weeks' unpaid parental leave during the first five years of the child's life or, if the child is adopted, until the fifth anniversary of adoption or the child's 18th birthday, whichever occurs sooner. If the child in question has been awarded a social security disability living allowance, the parents may take up to 18 weeks' unpaid parental leave until the child's 18th birthday. To qualify for parental leave, the parent must have been continuously employed by his or her employer for a minimum period of one year. Furthermore, the parent must supply his or her employer with evidence of childbirth or adoption and, where appropriate, evidence confirming the award of a disability living allowance. In the absence of any collective or workforce agreement to the contrary, an employee may not take more than four weeks' parental leave in any period of 12 consecutive months. Other procedures must also be followed. (*Sources:* ERA 1996, ss.76-80; **Maternity and Parental Leave, etc Regulations 1999**, as amended.)

part-time worker

A worker is a part-time worker for the purposes of the **Part-time Workers (Prevention of Less Favourable Treatment) Regulations 2000** if he or she is paid wholly or in part by reference to the time he or she works and, having regard to the custom and practice of the employer in relation to workers employed by the worker's employer under the same type of contract, is not identifiable as a full-time worker. Under the 2000 Regulations, a part-time worker has the legal right not to be treated less favourably than a comparable full-time worker (terms and conditions, rates of pay, etc) if both workers are employed by the same employer under the same type of contract, are engaged in the same or broadly similar work (having regard, where relevant, to whether they have a similar level of qualifications, skills and experience), and work or are based at the same establishment or (if there is no full-time worker working or based at that establishment who satisfies these requirements) works or is based at a different establishment with the same organisation and satisfies those requirements. (*Source:* PTWR 2000, regulation 2.)

paternity leave

Under the **Paternity and Adoption Leave Regulations 2002**, which came into force on 8 December 2002, employees who are the parents of a child born (or expected to be born) on or after 6 April 2003 have the qualified right to take either one week's paternity leave or two consecutive weeks' paternity leave within 56 days of the child's actual date of birth. That same qualified right extends to the parents of a child placed (or expected to be placed) with them for adoption on or after 6 April 2003. Most employees will also be entitled to Statutory Paternity Pay (SPP) during their absences from work on paternity leave. To qualify for paternity leave, an employee must (in a birth situation) have been continuously employed by his employer for a period of 26 weeks or more by the end of the 15th week before the mother's expected week of childbirth (EWC), or would have satisfied that requirement but for the fact that the child was either born before the beginning of that 14th week or was stillborn after 24 weeks of pregnancy, or has died. In an adoption situation he or she should have been continuously employed by his or her employer for 26 or more weeks by the end of the week in which the child's adopter is notified of having been matched with the child for adoption. An employee must also be able to demonstrate that he or she has or expects to have (apart from any responsibility of the child's mother or the adopter) the main responsibility for the child's upbringing. Certain other procedures and requirements must also be followed and satisfied. (*Source:* **Paternity and Adoption Leave Regulations 2002.**)

paternity pay   See *statutory paternity pay.*

pay in lieu of notice   There is nothing in law to prevent either party to a contract of employment from waiving his or her right to notice on any occasion or from accepting a payment in lieu of notice. (*Source:* ERA 1996, s.86(3).) On the other hand, and in the absence of any express term to the contrary, an employer does not have any common law or implied contractual right to require an employee who has resigned or been dismissed to take so-called "garden leave" (designed to prevent the employee taking up employment with a competitor during his or her notice period). In the absence of an express garden leave clause in an employee's contract, it is arguable that an employer's failure to provide the employee with work during his or her notice period is a repudiation of contract, entitling the employee to bring an action for damages arising out of that breach and providing him or her with a defence should he or she choose to take up employment with a competitor before that notice period expires. As decided law is not altogether clear on this point, employers would be well-advised to seek legal advice before incorporating garden leave clauses and other restrictive covenants in the contracts of employment of their (notably) key personnel. See also *fidelity and trust, duty of, implied term,* and *restrictive covenant.*

pay reference period   For the purposes of the **National Minimum Wage Regulations 1999**, the "pay reference period" is a month or, in the case of a worker who is paid wages by reference to a period shorter than a month, that shorter period. (*Source:* NMWR 1999, regulation 10.)

pension scheme trustees

Employees who are trustees of a relevant occupational pension scheme have the legal right to be permitted a reasonable amount of paid time off work to enable them to perform any of their duties as such trustees or to undergo training relevant to the performance of those duties. The expression "relevant occupational pension scheme" means an occupational pension scheme (as defined in s.1 of the **Pension Schemes Act 1993**) established under a trust. An employer who refuses or fails to permit such employees to take paid time off will be ordered by an employment tribunal to pay the employees such compensation as the tribunal considers to be just and equitable in the circumstances. (*Source:* ERA 1996, ss.58-60.)

pensions and pension schemes

The written statement of employment particulars necessarily issued to all new employees must (amongst other things) include particulars of any terms and conditions relating to pensions and pension schemes. Alternatively, it must refer the employee to the provisions of some other document that is readily accessible to the employee and explains those particulars in more detail. If the employer has no occupational pension scheme, the statement must say as much. (*Source:* ERA 1996, s.1.)

permitted reasons for dismissal

When responding to a complaint of unfair dismissal before an employment tribunal, the onus is on the employer to show the reason or (if more than one, the principal reason) for the employee's dismissal and that it was either a reason relating to the employee's capability or qualifications, conduct, the illegality of contin-ued employment, or redundancy — "or some other substantial reason of a kind such as to justify the dismissal of an employee holding the position the employee held". (*Source*: ERA 1996, s.98.) See also *inadmissible reasons for dismissal.*

personal data

The **Data Protection Act 1998** defines "personal data" as meaning data relating to a living individual (the data subject) who can be identified either from that data or from any other information or document which is in (or is likely to come into) the possession of the data controller (in this context, the employer). In short, "personal data" means any data (from whatever source) which relates to a named or readily identifiable individual, including any expression of opinion and any indication of the intentions of the data controller (or any other person) in respect of that individual — whether contained in (or appended to) a letter, memorandum, report, certificate or other document, or held in a paper-based file, on computer, or by any other automated or non-automated means.

picketing

"It is lawful for a person, in contemplation or furtherance of a trade dispute, to attend at or near his own place of work, or, if he is an official of a trade union, at or near the place of work of a member of that union whom he is accompanying and whom he represents, for the purpose only of peacefully obtaining or communicating information, or peacefully persuading any person to work or abstain from work". Picketing is not actionable in tort if it meets these criteria. But it is actionable as a form of industrial action if it does not have the support of a ballot or is done in order to put pressure on an employer to dismiss a non-union member (or to discriminate against him) or to "persuade" the employer not to hire non-union workers.(*Source:* TULRA 1992, s.207 and ss.219-222.)

Practical guidance for employers, workers or members of the public who may be affected by a picket or any associated activities is to be found in the Code of Practice: *Picketing* (Ref. URN 96/618), copies of which are available from the DTI's Publications Orderline on 0870 1502 500 (e-mail: publications@dti.gsi.gov.uk).

PILON   See *pay in lieu of notice.*

political fund   Trade union members have the legal right not to contribute to their union's political fund (ie a fund set aside for political purposes), and will be exempt from contributing to that fund once they have served written notice to that effect on the union in question. An employer who operates a "check-off" system for the deduction of union dues, who has received written notice from an employee who is a trade union member certifying that he or she is exempt from contributing to the union's political fund, must ensure (as soon as is reasonably practicable) that no amount representing a contribution to that fund is deducted from the employee's wages or salary. (*Source:* TULRA 1992, ss.82–87.)

political affiliation   See *Fair Employment and Treatment (Northern Ireland) Order 1998.*

posted workers   UK workers sent (ie posted) by their employers to carry out temporary work in another EU Member State (and vice versa) must be paid no less than the national minimum wage applicable to comparable workers in the "host" state; must not be required to work longer hours than those laid down in the legislation of that Member State; must have the same minimum rest breaks and rest periods; and must enjoy no less favourable "hard-core" terms and conditions of employment. This requirement is to be found in EU Directive 96/71/EC of 16 December 1996 "concerning the posting of workers in the framework of the provision of services". Temporary work is work which is unlikely to last for longer than 12 months. (*Sources:* Council Directive 96/71/EC of 16 December 1996; **Equal Opportunities (Employment Legislation) (Territorial Limits) Regulations 1999**.)

pregnant employees The statutory rights enjoyed by a pregnant employee include the qualified right to be paid her normal wages or salary if suspended from work on maternity grounds; the right to be permitted a reasonable amount of paid time off work for ante-natal care; the right to be provided with suitable rest facilities for use during the working day; the right to be transferred from night work to suitable day work if work at night poses a risk to her health and safety (or that of her unborn child); and the right not to be discriminated against, selected for redundancy, or subjected to any other detriment for exercising or asserting her statutory rights (including her right to maternity leave and her right to return to work after childbirth). See *antenatal care, maternity rights, new or expectant mothers, night work: new or expectant mothers, risk assessment* and *suspension on maternity grounds*.

principal statement See *written statement of employment particulars*.

privacy, right to See *European Convention on Human Rights*.

protected disclosure The expression "protected disclosure" means a qualifying disclosure which is made by a worker in accordance with the "Protected Disclosure" provisions of the **Employment Rights Act 1996** (as inserted by the **Public Interest Disclosure Act 1998**).

protection of wages See *deductions from pay*.

public duties, time off for Employees who are justices of the peace or members of:
- a local authority
- a statutory tribunal (eg an employment tribunal)

- a police authority
- the service authority for the National Criminal Intelligence Service
- the service authority for the National Crime Squad
- a board of prison visitors or a prison visiting committee
- a relevant health authority
- a relevant education body
- the Environment Agency or the Scottish Environment Protection Agency
- a Scottish water and sewerage authority
- a water industry consultative committee
- the General Teaching Council for England or the General Teaching Council for Wales

have the legal right (regardless of their length of service at the material time) to be permitted a reasonable amount of time off work during their normal working hours to enable them to carry out their extra-curricular activities. Although the relevant provisions in the **Employment Rights Act 1996** do not state whether employees exercising their right to time off work in the circumstances described above are or are not entitled to be paid during their absence from work on such occasions, the Employment Appeal Tribunal has expressed the view that an employer's refusal to pay an employee who needs to take time off work to attend to his or her public duties could prove to be a deterrent sufficient to prevent that employee exercising that statutory right.

In *Corner v Buckingham County Council* [1978] ICR 836, Slynn J remarked that "in considering where there has been refusal to grant time off, the employment tribunal can look at the conditions subject to which an employer is prepared to grant time off (including conditions relating to pay) and could say that they really amounted to a refusal to allow time to be taken". (*Source:* ERA 1996, ss.50-51.)

Public Interest Disclosure Act 1998

Under the 1998 Act (commonly referred to as the "Whistle Blower's Act") workers who make so-called "protected disclosures" have the legal right not to be dismissed, selected for redundancy, victimised, discriminated against, or subjected to any other detriment for having done so. Any term in an employee's (or other worker's) contract that purports to override or undermine that right is void and unenforceable. The expression "protected disclosure" means a qualifying disclosure, that is to say, a disclosure concerning an employer's alleged criminal activities, failure to pay the correct national minimum wage, breaches of health and safety legislation (putting other people's lives at risk), damage to the environment, attempts to defraud the Inland Revenue or HM Custom and Excise; and so on.

To enjoy the protection afforded by the 1998 Act (whose provisions have since been incorporated into the **Employment Rights Act 1996**), a worker must have a reasonable belief in the truth of his or her allegations; must first report the matter to his or her employer or a person nominated by the employer to deal with such matters (in accordance with procedures established by the employer for this purpose), or to the person responsible for the alleged wrongdoing, or *in extremis*, to the relevant enforcing authority (such as the Health and Safety Executive, the Inland Revenue, HM Customs and Excise, the Environment Agency, the Audit Commission or the Office of Fair Trading). There is no upper limit on the amount of compensation payable to a worker who is dismissed or subjected to any other detriment for

117

having made a qualifying disclosure. **A Guide to the Public Interest Disclosure Act 1998** (Ref. URN 99/511) is available from the DTI's Publications Orderline (tel: 0870 1502 500) or may be accessed and downloaded from website www.dti.gov.uk. (*Source:* ERA 1996, ss.47B, 103A, 105 and Part IVA.)

Q

qualifications

In relation to an employee, "qualifications" means any degree, diploma or other academic, technical or professional qualification relevant to the position that employee held. A dismissal relating to the capability or qualifications of an employee is a permitted reason for dismissal. (*Source:* ERA 1996, s.98.)

qualifying disclosure

See *Public Interest Disclosure Act 1998*.

questions and replies

Employees (or job applicants), who believe that they have been unlawfully discriminated against by their employer (or would-be employer), on grounds of sex, race or disability, may submit a written questionnaire to the relevant person or organisation asking for an explanation for its apparently unlawful actions. The answers provided by the employer in the completed questionnaire are admissible in evidence in proceedings before an employment tribunal, as is an employer's refusal or failure to complete or return the questionnaire within a reasonable time. The forms prescribed for these purposes are, respectively, SD74 (sex), RR65 (race) and DL56 (disability), and are available (with accompanying explanatory notes) from offices of the Equal Opportunities Commission, the Commission for Racial Equality or the Disability Rights Commission. (*Sources:* **Sex Discrimination (Questions and Replies) Order 1975; Race**

Relations (Questions and Replies) Order 1977.)
See also *disability discrimination, racial discrimination* and *sex discrimination*.

Note: Once s.42 of the **Employment Act 2002** comes into force (6 April 2003), importing a new s.7B into the **Equal Pay Act 1970**, a similar "questions and replies" facility will be available to persons who believe they have claims under s.1 of the 1970 Act.

R

racial discrimination

It is unlawful for employers to discriminate against job applicants on racial grounds in the arrangements they make for the purpose of determining who should be offered employment; or in the terms on which they offer them that employment; or by refusing or deliberately omitting to offer them that employment. It is also unlawful for employers to discriminate against existing employees on racial grounds in the terms of employment they afford them; or in the way they afford them access to opportunities for promotion, transfer, training (or to any other benefits, facilities or services), or by refusing or deliberately omitting to offer them access to them; or by dismissing them or subjecting them to any other detriment. However, denying a person access (or promotion or transfer) to a particular job on racial grounds is *prima facie* permissible if being of a particular racial group is a genuine occupational qualification for that job for reasons of authenticity (eg employment as a waiter in an Indian or Chinese restaurant); or if the holder of the job provides persons of that same racial group with personal services promoting their welfare and those services can most effectively be provided by a person of that racial group. (*Source:* **Race Relations Act 1976**.)

racial grounds   "means any of the following grounds, namely colour, race, nationality or ethnic or national origins". (*Source:* RRA 1976, s.3.)

racial group   "means a group of persons defined by reference to colour, race, nationality or ethnic or national origins, and references to a person's racial group refer to any racial group into which he [or she] falls." The fact that a racial group comprises two or more distinct racial groups does not prevent it from constituting a particular racial group for the purposes of the **Race Relations Act 1976**. (*Source:* RRA 1976, s.3.)

recognised independent trade union   See *trade union recognition*.

redundancy payment   See *statutory redundancy pay*.

re-engagement   On a finding of unfair dismissal, an employment tribunal may direct the respondent employer either to reinstate or re-engage the employee in question. An order for re-engagement is an order directing the employer (or a successor or associated employer) to re-engage the employee in employment comparable to that from which he or she was dismissed, or other suitable employment. An employer who refuses or fails to comply (or comply fully) with an order for re-engagement will be ordered to pay the employee an additional award of compensation of between 26 and 52 weeks' pay. (*Source:* ERA 1996, ss.113-117.) See also *reinstatement*.

references   Employers are under no legal obligation to provide former employees with references. But, if they do so, according to the *High Court in Lawton v BOC Transhield Ltd* [1987] IRLR 404, they owe a duty to that employee to take reasonable care to ensure that the opinions expressed in it are based on accurate facts and, in so far as the reference itself states facts, that those facts are themselves accurate. When an employer approaches another employer for information and opinions about one of the latter's employees (past or present), said the court, it should be self-evident that the employee in question has proffered his or her former employer's name as referee, that the employee is being seriously considered for employment elsewhere, that the employee is relying on his or her former employer to get the facts right, and that an adverse report would almost certainly result in the employee being taken off the short list or remaining unemployed for an unspecified period. In other words, the duty of care extends not only to the person seeking the relevant information but also to the employee in respect of whom that information is sought.

Under the "right of access to personal data" provisions of the **Data Protection Act 1998**, employees have no legal right to see or take copies of references issued by their present employers for employment or education purposes. They do have the qualified right to see references provided by former employers (subject to any duty of confidentiality owed by the employer to that other employer).

Rehabilitation of Offenders Act 1974

This enactment effectively entitles a person with one or more criminal convictions to withhold information about those convictions from an employer (or would-be employer) once those convictions become "spent". However, withholding details of criminal convictions (spent or otherwise) is not permissible if the person in question is seeking employment in an excepted occupation or profession (eg doctor, nurse, veterinary surgeon, chemist, teacher, controller or manager of an insurance company, dealer in securities, chartered or certified accountant and work involving the care or supervision of young persons under 18). A conviction becomes spent if the person in question is not again convicted of an indictable offence within a specified number of years (usually between 5 and 10). However, a sentence of imprisonment for life, or a sentence of imprisonment, youth custody, etc for a term exceeding 30 months does not become spent; nor does a sentence of preventive detention or a sentence of detention during Her Majesty's pleasure.

Reinstatement
On a finding of unfair dismissal, an employment tribunal may direct the respondent employer either to reinstate or re-engage the employee in question. An order for reinstatement is an order directing the employer to treat the employee in question in all respects as if he or she had not been dismissed (in other words, to reinstate the employee in the job he or she held when dismissed). An employer who refuses or fails to comply (or comply fully) with an order for reinstatement will be ordered to pay the employee an additional award of compensation of between 26 and 52 weeks' pay. (*Source:* ERA 1996, ss.113-117.) See also *re-engagement*.

relevant filing system
"In the context of the **Data Protection Act 1998**, the term 'relevant filing system' means any set of information relating to individuals to the extent that, although the information is not processed by means of equipment operating automatically in response to instructions given for that purpose, the set is structured either by reference to individuals, or by reference to criteria relating to individuals, in such a way that specific information relating to a particular individual is readily accessible" (ie documents containing personal data about individuals held in a manual

or paper-based filing system). Under the "subject access provisions" of the **Data Protection Act 1998** (and subject to certain transitional provisions relating to paper-based files developed before 24 October 1998), employees and other workers have the right to see and take copies of documents containing personal data about them that are held in both their employers' computerised and paper-based filing systems. (*Source:* DPA 1998.) See also *data protection* and *personal data*.

relevant transfer Means a transfer to which the **Transfer of Undertakings (Protection of Employment) Regulations 1981** applies (TUPE regulation 1). See also *transfers of undertakings*.

religious beliefs Save for Northern Ireland, discrimination on grounds of a person's religious beliefs or affiliations is not yet unlawful in the UK. However, that situation will change once the UK Government implements Council Directive 2000/78/EC of 2 December 2000 which outlaws discrimination in employment, not only on grounds of religion or belief, but also on grounds of age, disability and sexual orientation. Member States have until 2 December 2003 to implement the Directive's provisions relating to discrimination on grounds of religion or belief and sexual orientation. See also *Fair Employment and Treatment (Northern Ireland) Order 1998*.

representatives See *appropriate representatives*.

representatives of employee safety Any group of employees that is not represented by trade union-appointed safety representatives under the **Health and Safety (Consultation with Employees) Regulations 1996 and Safety Representatives and Safety Committee Regulations 1977** has the right to elect one or more member(s) of the group to represent its interests in consultations with its employer. Such persons are referred to as "representatives of employee safety". For the most part, they enjoy the same statutory rights as their trade union-appointed contemporaries, including the right to paid time off work to carry out their functions and/or to attend appropriate safety training courses. See also *safety representatives* and *time off work: general.*

rest breaks

An adult worker is entitled to a minimum 20-minute break during any working day or shift lasting, or expected to last, for more than six hours. A young person under the age of 18 is entitled to a minimum 30-minute break in every working day or shift lasting (or expected to last) for more than four-and-a-half hours. (*Source:* WTR 1998, regulations 12 and 21.)

rest facilities: new and expectant mothers

Employers are duty-bound to provide suitable rest facilities for use during working hours by those of their employees who are pregnant or breastfeeding or who have given birth within the previous six months. To be suitable, the facility must afford a measure of privacy; be clean and well-ventilated; be equipped with a wash basin, toilet and one or more day beds or comfortable chairs or be situated within easy walking distance of washrooms and toilets used by other (female) employees. The nature, extent and suitability of such a facility (which may comprise a dedicated room or a curtained-off area set apart for use by new or expectant mothers) will depend in large part on the size of the employing organisation. A failure to provide these facilities is an offence for which the penalty on summary conviction is a fine of up to £5000. (*Source:* **Workplace (Health, Safety and Welfare) Regulations 1992**, regulation 25.)

rest periods (daily and weekly)

Under the **Working Time Regulations 1998**, every adult worker (other than a shift worker) is entitled to a rest period of 11 consecutive hours between each working day, and an uninterrupted weekly rest period of at least 24 hours in each seven-day period. The weekly rest period may be averaged over a two-week period, ensuring that an adult worker has at least two work-free rest days (or periods) in every fortnight. An adult worker's entitlement to rest may be modified or excluded by a collective or workforce agreement (so long as the worker in question is permitted to take "an equivalent period of compensatory rest" whenever possible). These requirements do not apply to workers who have a measure of control over the number of hours they work and whose working hours are not monitored or controlled by their employers. Nor do they apply to workers in excluded sectors (notably, the transport industry). (*Source:* WTR 1998, regulations 10, 11, 21 and 22.)

Young workers under the age of 18 are entitled to an uninterrupted daily work-free rest period of 12 hours in every 24 hours, and to a rest period of a minimum two days in every period of seven consecutive days. There is no provision for the averaging of that two-day weekly rest period. However, the weekly rest period may be reduced to 36 hours if justified "for technical or organisational reasons". (WTR 1998.)

restraint of trade   See *restrictive covenant.*

restrictive covenant   A covenant incorporated into the contracts of employment of (typically) key employees, reminding them of their implied contractual duty (a duty that persists after their employment has ended) not to divulge to unauthorised third parties any confidential information concerning their employer's business activities (pricing policies, marketing strategies, trade secrets, chemical formulae, etc) acquired by them during the course of their employment. A restrictive covenant may also impose a duty on such employees not to compete with their employer after their employment has ended or accept employment with another employer in the same trade or industry (ideally for a limited period and within a clearly defined geographical area).

A covenant in "restraint of trade" is *prima facie* void and will not be enforced by the courts unless it is shown to be reasonable as between the parties and in the public interest. It is for the employer to demonstrate that it is reasonable in area and time in order to reasonably protect its business interests. A claim that such a restriction is not in the public interest must be proved by the employee (*Spencer v Marchington* [1988] IRLR 392, HC). A covenant, construed by the courts as giving the employer more protection than is necessary or was intended will fail unless it is possible to apply the so called "blue pencil" test, ie by deleting the offending sentences or clauses without distorting the meaning of the remainder (the Court of Appeal in *Attwood v Lamont* [1920] 3 KB 571). See also *fidelity and trust, duty of.*

retail employment   In the context of a worker's statutory right not to suffer unauthorised deduction from his or her wages (notably in relation to cash shortages and stock deficiencies) the term "retail employment", in relation to a worker, means employment involving (whether or not on a regular basis) the carrying out by the worker of retail transactions (ie the sale or supply of goods or the supply of services, including financial services) directly with members of the public or with fellow workers or other individuals in their personal capacities, or the collection by the worker of amounts payable in connection with retail transactions carried out by other persons directly with members of the public or with fellow workers or other individuals in their personal capacities. (*Source:* ERA 1996, s.17.)

return to work

An employee exercising his or her legal right to return to work after ordinary adoption leave, ordinary maternity leave, parental leave or paternity leave, has the right to do so in the job he or she held before that period of leave began. An employee returning to work after additional adoption leave or additional maternity leave has that same right unless it is not reasonably practicable for the employer to permit the employee to return to work in his or her original job, in which case the employee has the right to return to work in a suitable alternative job (with no loss of seniority or pension rights) and on terms and conditions no less favourable to the employee than those that prevailed immediately before his or her period of leave began. An employee who takes four or more weeks' parental leave immediately after additional adoption or maternity leave may likewise forfeit his or her right to return to work in his or her original job, so long as the employer can establish that it was not reasonably practicable to permit the employee to return to work in that original job at the end of the additional adoption or maternity leave period and that it is still not reasonably practicable to permit the employee to do so. (*Sources:* **Maternity and Parental Leave, etc Regulations 1999** (as amended); and the **Paternity and Adoption Leave Regulations 2002**.)

risk assessment

Every employer, regardless of the size of its business or undertaking, is duty-bound to carry out a risk assessment exercise to identify the risks to the health and safety of its employees and the risks to the health and safety of other persons (eg members of the public, customers, clients, trades people, etc) arising out of, or in connection with, the way in which the business is conducted or managed. Having identified those risks, the employer must take appropriate steps to minimise or eliminate them. In organisations with five or more people "on the payroll" the employers must document the significant findings of the assessment, and the group of employees identified by it as being especially at risk. The exercise must be repeated as often as may be necessary in the light of changes in working practices or the introduction of new plant and equipment, production processes or dangerous chemicals and substances.

When conducting their risk assessments, employers must take account of the relative inexperience, lack of maturity and the (at times) cavalier attitudes or indifference of young persons under the age of 18 to workplace hazards. Employers who employ women of child-bearing age must, likewise, assess the risks confronting new or expectant mothers (or their children or developing foetuses) from any processes or working conditions, or from any physical, biological or chemical agents to which they are exposed while at work. If such risks cannot be avoided, the employer must either alter a new or expectant mother's working conditions or hours of work or, if doing so would not avoid the risks, either transfer her to suitable alternative work or suspend her from work for so long as is necessary to avoid such risks. (*Source:* MHSAWR 1999, regulations 3 and 16.) See also *new or expectant mothers* and *young person*.

S

safety committee   If asked to do so by two or more trade union-appointed safety representatives, an employer is duty-bound, in accordance with the **Safety Representatives and Safety Committees Regulations 1977**, to establish a safety committee having the function of keeping under review the measures taken to ensure the health and safety at work of its employees and such other functions as are prescribed in those Regulations. (*Source:* HASAWA 1974, s.2(7).)

safety representatives

An independent trade union recognised by an employer as having bargaining rights in respect of some or all of the employer's employees has the legal right to appoint one or more safety representatives from among its members to represent the interests of those employees in matters affecting their health and safety at work. Employers, for their part, have a duty to consult any such representatives with a view to the making and maintenance of arrangements which will enable them and their employees to co-operate effectively in promoting and developing measures to ensure the health and safety at work of those employees, and in checking the effectiveness of such measures. The number of safety representatives to be appointed is a matter for discussion and agreement between the employer and the trade unions in question. (*Sources:* HASAWA 1974, s.2(4)-(7); **Safety Representatives and Safety Committees Regulations 1977.**) See also *safety committee* and *time off work: general.*

same type of contract

Under the **Part-time Workers (Prevention of Less Favourable Treatment) Regulations 2000**, a part-time worker (whether employee or otherwise) has the legal right not to be treated less favourably than a comparable full-time worker (that is to say, a worker who is employed under the "same type of contract" as that part-time worker). The Regulations state that workers employed under the following types of contract are not employed under the same type of contract:

    (a) employees employed under a contract that is not a contract of apprenticeship

(b) employees employed under a contract of apprenticeship

(c) workers who are not employees

(d) any other description of worker that it is reasonable for the employer to treat differently from other workers on the ground that workers of that description have a different kind of contract.

Thus, (a) is not the same type of contract as (b); (c) is not the same type of contract as (a); (b) not the same as (c); and so on. (*Source*: PTWR 2000, regulation 2.) See also *comparable full-time worker* and *part-time worker*.

self-employed person

In law, a self-employed person is a person employed under a contract for services — that is to say, a person who is in business on his or her own account, who supplies his or her own workers, who presents an invoice and charges an agreed fee for services rendered, who is paid the same regardless of the length of time to complete a job or work, who provides his or her own tools, plant and equipment, pays for the materials needed to complete a job, accepts a large degree of financial risk, prepares annual accounts for submission to the Inland Revenue, pays his or her own tax and National Insurance Contributions (NICs), is VAT registered (where necessary); and so on.

The degree of control and direction exercised by the client employer over a worker who claims to be self-employed is also an important factor to consider. The greater the degree of control, the less likely it is that the worker is self-employed. Self-employed persons do not enjoy the statutory rights afforded to employees and other workers under contemporary employment legislation. Should there be a dispute, in proceedings before an employment tribunal, concerning the true status of a worker claiming access to such rights, it will be for the tribunal to compare factors indicating employment with those indicating self-employment and to make a decision on that basis before the worker's claim or complaint can be heard. In the context of PAYE tax and NICs, employers who are doubtful about the true status of a worker who purports to be self-employed would be well advised to contact their local Tax Enquiry Centre, Tax Office or Contributions Agency Office.

sex discrimination Under the provisions of the **Sex Discrimination Act 1975**, it is unlawful for an employer to discriminate against a woman (or man) on grounds of her sex (or marital status) by refusing or deliberately omitting to offer her employment; by applying to her a requirement or condition with which fewer women than men can comply; by employing her on terms and conditions less favourable to her than those offered to a man doing the same or similar work; by denying her access (or equal access) to opportunities for promotion, transfer or training; by victimising her or subjecting her to any detriment because of her sex or marital status; or by dismissing her or selecting her for redundancy because she is a woman. (*Source:* SDA 1975, Parts I and II.) See also *direct discrimination, gender reassignment, genuine occupational qualification, indirect discrimination* and *sexual harassment.*

sexual harassment "Unwanted conduct of a sexual nature, or other conduct based on sex, affecting the dignity of women and men at work, including any kind of unwanted physical, verbal or non-verbal behaviour which offends the dignity of the person, including: physical contact (ranging from unnecessary touching, patting, pinching, and brushing against a person's body to molestation, assault and coercing sexual intercourse) sexually-suggestive gestures, leering, whistling

131

or over-familiar comments about a person's appearance physical attributes, or dress; insults or ridicule based on a person's sex or sexual orientation; displays of pornographic or sexually-suggestive pictures, objects or written material; suggestions that sexual favours may further a person's career (or that a refusal may damage it); and decisions based on her or his willingness or refusal to offer sexual favours". (*Source*: EU Code of Practice (COM 91 1397 final) *Combating Sexual Harassment and Protecting the Dignity of Women and Men at Work*). In *Strathclyde Regional Council v Porcelli* [1986] IRLR 134, the Court of Session characterised sexual harassment as "a particularly degrading and unacceptable form of treatment which it must be taken to have been the intention of Parliament to restrain". The **Sex Discrimination Act 1975** nevertheless contains no direct reference to sexual harassment. It remains for victims of sexual harassment in the workplace to persuade an employment tribunal that their treatment at the hands of their tormentors was tantamount to unlawful direct discrimination on the grounds of sex (contrary to s.1(1)(a) of the 1975 Act) and that they were "subjected to a detriment" as a result of that treatment. (*Source:* SDA 1975, s.1.) See also *harassment, alarm and distress*.

sexual orientation Discrimination on grounds of an employee's sexual orientation is not yet unlawful in the UK. However, such discrimination will be unlawful once the Government implements Council Directive 2000/78/EC of 2 December 2000 which outlaws discrimination in employment on grounds of age, religion or belief, disability or sexual orientation. Member States have until 2 December 2003 to implement the Directive's provisions relating to discrimination on grounds of sexual orientation, religion or belief.

shop worker

Means an employee who, under his or her contract of employment is, or may be, required to do shop work (ie work in or about a shop in England or Wales on a day on which the shop is open for the serving of customers). A "shop", for these purposes, includes any premises where any retail trade or business is carried on but does not include a catering business (such as a public house, restaurant or cafeteria, or other premises in which meals, refreshments or intoxicating liquor are sold for immediate consumption on the premises). (*Source:* ERA 1996, s.232.) See also *Sunday working*.

short-time working and lay-offs

See *lay-offs and short-time working*.

sick pay

The written statement of employment particulars necessarily issued to every new employee must (amongst other things) include particulars of any terms and conditions relating to incapacity for work due to sickness or injury, including any provision for sick pay, or refer the employee to some other readily-accessible document (such as a staff or works handbook) that explains those particulars in more detail. If the employer does not operate an occupational sick pay scheme, that fact must be stated in the written statement. (*Source:* ERA 1996, s.1(4)(d) and 2.) See also *statutory sick pay*.

some other substantial reason

An employee may lawfully be dismissed on grounds of lack of capability or qualifications, misconduct, redundancy, the illegality of his or her continued employment or for "some other substantial reason of a kind such as to justify the dismissal of an employee holding the position the employee held" (eg a refusal to come to terms with changes in technology, the adoption of new working practices or a transfer from day work to shift work accepted by most other members of the workforce). When responding to a complaint of unfair dismissal it is for the employer to demonstrate the reason (or, if more than one, the principal reason) for the complainant employee's dismissal. It will then be for the tribunal to determine whether or not the employer had acted reasonably and fairly in treating that reason as a sufficient reason for dismissing the employee in question. (*Source:* ERA 1996, s.98.)

statement of initial employment particulars

See *written statement of employment particulars.*

statutory adoption pay

An employee who qualifies for adoption leave, and who has average weekly earnings equal to, or greater than, the lower earnings limit (LEL) for National Insurance Contributions (NICs) purposes (£77 a week), will normally qualify for up to 26 weeks' statutory adoption pay (SAP) during his or her ordinary adoption pay period. The adoption pay period is the period that begins on the day immediately following the day on which an employee begins his or her ordinary adoption leave. The rate of SAP is £100 a week or 90 per cent of the employee's average weekly earnings, whichever is the lower of those amounts. (*Sources:***Statutory Paternity Pay and Statutory Adoption Pay (General) Regulations 2002; Statutory Paternity Pay and Statutory Adoption Pay (Weekly Rates) Regulations 2002.**) See also *adoption leave.*

Employers who have lawfully paid SAP to an employee will (as is the case with payments of SMP and SPP) be able to recover an amount equal to 92 per cent of the amount paid by deducting it from PAYE tax and NICs routinely remitted to the Inland Revenue at the end of each income tax month. Small employers (the total of whose NICs did not exceed £40,000 during the preceding tax year) will, for their part, be able to recover 100 per cent of the amount of SAP paid, plus a further 4.5 per cent to recoup the additional NICs paid on such payments. These figures are reviewed every year.

statutory maternity pay A woman qualifies for up to 18 weeks' statutory maternity pay (SMP) during her maternity pay period (or, if her expected week of childbirth (EWC) begins, or began, on or after 6 April 2003, up to 26 weeks' SMP during that same period) if her average weekly earnings at the end of the 15th week before her EWC were equal to, or greater than the current lower earnings limit (LEL) (£77) for National Insurance Contributions (NICs) purposes. The maternity pay period is the period of up to 18 weeks that begins on the Sunday of the week immediately following the day on which the employee began her maternity leave; or, in the case of an employee whose EWC begins or began on or after 6 April 2003, the period of up to 26 weeks beginning on the day immediately following the day on which she began her maternity leave. From 6 April 2003, that LEL increases from £75 to £77 a week.

There are two rates of SMP, the higher rate and the lower rate. The higher rate is an amount equivalent to nine-tenths of the employee's average weekly earnings and is payable for each of the first six weeks of the maternity pay period. The lower rate, payable for the each of the remaining up to 12 (or 20) weeks of that same period is £75 a week, rising (from 6 April 2003, subject to certain transitional provisions) to £100 a week or 90 per cent of her average weekly earnings, whichever is the lower of those amounts. (*Source:* **Statutory Maternity Pay (General) Regulations 1986; Social Security, Statutory Maternity Pay and Statutory Sick Pay (Miscellaneous Amendments) Regulations 2002.**)

Employers who have lawfully paid SMP to an employee will (as is the case with payments of SAP and SPP) be able to recover an amount equal to 92 per cent of the amount paid by deducting it from PAYE tax and NICs routinely remitted to the Inland Revenue at the end of each income tax month. Small employers (the total of whose NICs did not exceed £40,000 during the preceding tax year) will be able to recover 100 per cent of the amount of SMP paid, plus a further 4.5 per cent to recoup the additional NICs paid on such payments. These figures are reviewed every year. (*Source:* **Statutory Maternity Pay (Compensation of Employers) Amendment Regulations 2002**.) See also *additional maternity leave, ordinary maternity leave, rights during, and maternity rights.*

statutory paternity pay

An eligible employee will qualify for statutory paternity pay (SPP) during his or her absence from work on paternity leave if he or she has average weekly earnings equal to or greater than the current Lower Earnings Limit (LEL) for National Insurance Contributions (NICs) purposes. For 2003/04, that LEL is £77 per week. Statutory paternity pay (SPP) is payable at the same standard rate as statutory maternity pay (SMP), ie £100 a week or 90 per cent of the employee's average weekly earnings at the time, whichever is the lower of those amounts. Employers who have lawfully paid SPP to an employee will (as is the case with payments of SAP and SMP) be able to recover an amount equal to 92 per cent of the amount paid by deducting it from PAYE tax and NICs routinely remitted to the Inland Revenue at the end of each income tax month. Small employers (the total of whose NICs did not exceed £40,000 during the preceding tax year) will be able to recover 100 per cent of the amount of SPP paid, plus a further 4.5 per cent to recoup the additional NICs paid on such payments. These figures are reviewed every year. See also *statutory maternity pay.*

statutory redundancy pay

A redundant employee with two or more years' continuous service at the effective date of termination of his or her contract of employment (excluding any period of service that began before his or her 18th birthday) is entitled to a statutory redundancy payment, calculated as follows:

- one-and-a-half weeks' pay for each year of employment in which he or she was not below the age of 41
- one week's pay for each year of employment in which he or she was below the age of 41 but not below the age of 22
- a half week's pay for each year of employment in which he or she was below the age of 22 but not below the age of 18.

Service in excess of 20 years (reckoned backwards from the date on which the employee's employment ended) may lawfully be ignored, as may earnings in excess of £260 per week (which latter amount is reviewed each year). It follows that the maximum statutory redundancy payment payable to an employee with 20 or more years' service after the age of 41 is £7800 (20 x 1.5 x £260). In the case of an employee made redundant after his or her 64th birthday, the amount payable may be reduced by one-twelfth for each complete calendar month by which his or her age exceeds 64. Thus, a redundant employee aged 64 years and eight months on the termination of his or her employment can expect to have the redundancy payment otherwise payable to him or her reduced by eight-twelfths. (*Source:* ERA 1996, s.162.)

statutory sick pay (SSP)

An eligible employee who is (or is deemed to be) incapacitated for work for four or more consecutive whole days (including Saturdays, Sundays, rest days and bank and public holidays) will qualify to be paid up to 28 weeks' statutory sick pay (SSP)during any single period of incapacity for work (PIW). SSP is payable only in respect of the fourth and subsequent qualifying days in a PIW, the first three qualifying days in that period being unpaid waiting days. Qualifying days are either days of the week in which an employee is contractually required to work or such other days as are agreed in discussions between employers and their employees as being qualifying days. The current (2003/04) weekly rate of SSP is £64.35; the daily rate being the weekly amount divided by the number of qualifying days in that week.(*Source:* **Statutory Sick Pay (General) Regulations 1982** (as amended).) See also *sick pay.*

stock deficiency   Means a stock deficiency arising in the course of retail transactions. Deductions from the wages of a worker in retail employment (or a demands for payment from such a worker) on account of stock deficiencies (or cash shortages) are permissible if, but only if, there is an express term in that worker's contract (signed at the time his or her employment began) authorising such deductions; or if the worker has previously agreed (in writing) to any such deduction or payment and the circumstances in which such deductions or payments may be made. (*Source:* ERA 1996, ss.17-22). For further details, see *cash shortages.*

strike action   See *industrial action.*

study and training, time off for   See *time off work: general.*

summary dismissal   Employees guilty of gross misconduct, amounting to a serious breach of their contract of employment, are liable to be summarily dismissed, without benefit of the notice to which they are otherwise entitled to terminate that contract of employment. However, as is pointed out in ACAS Code of Practice 1: *Disciplinary and Grievance Procedures*, the word "summary" is not necessarily synonymous with "instant". Allegations of gross misconduct should nonetheless be investigated thoroughly before a decision is taken to dismiss the employee in question. If those investigations are likely to take a little time, the employee should be suspended from work on full pay until the issue is resolved. See also *breach of contract*.

Sunday working

Shop and betting workers (in their capacities as employees) have the right not to be dismissed, selected for redundancy, penalised or subjected to any other detriment (eg a cut in pay or a denial of overtime working) for refusing to work on Sundays. These rights prevail regardless of their ages, working hours or length of service. Shop workers who first started work with their employers before 26 August 1994, and betting workers who first started work with their employers before 3 January 1995, have automatic access to those rights (unless they subsequently agree to opt-in to Sunday work). These are known as "protected workers". Shop and betting workers, whose periods of employment began after those dates, may opt-out of Sunday work by giving their employers three months' advance written notice of their intentions. During that notice period they must continue to work on Sundays (if asked to do so) and may not be dismissed, selected for redundancy or otherwise penalised for exercising that right. Furthermore, the right of shop workers and betting workers to opt-out of Sunday work is a continuing one. Any shop or betting worker who opts-in to Sunday working has the right to opt-out again on giving the prescribed three months' advance written notice. However, these rights do not extend to shop and betting workers who have been specifically employed to work only on Sundays. (*Source:* ERA 1996, Part IV and ss.45, 101 and 105.) See also *betting work, betting worker* and *shop worker*.

supplementary award

If the evidence before an employment tribunal in an unfair dismissal case reveals that the employer provided an internal procedure for appealing against dismissal, that the employee had been reminded in writing of his or her right of appeal, but nonetheless failed to take advantage of that right, the tribunal may reduce the amount of any compensatory award otherwise payable to that employee by the equivalent of up to two weeks' pay. If, on the other hand, the evidence shows that the employer had prevented the employee lodging an appeal, the amount of that compensatory award may be increased by the equivalent of up to two weeks' pay. (*Source:* ERA 1996, s.127A.)

suspension on maternity grounds

An employee is suspended from work on maternity grounds if, in consequence of any relevant requirement or relevant recommendation, she is suspended from work by her employer on the ground that she is pregnant, has recently given birth or is breastfeeding a child. The expression "relevant requirement" means a requirement imposed by or under the **Management of Health and Safety at Work Regulations 1999**, the **Ionising Radiations Regulations 1999**, and the **Control of Lead at Work Regulations 2002**. "Relevant recommendation" means a recommendation in a code of practice approved under s.16 of the **Health and Safety at Work, etc Act 1974**. An employee who has been suspended from work on maternity grounds (regardless of her length of service at the material time) is entitled to be paid her normal remuneration while so suspended unless her employer has offered her suitable alternative work to do (on terms and conditions no less favourable to her than those that applied to her in her regular work) and she has unreasonably refused to perform that work. (*Source:* ERA 1996, ss.66-68.)

suspension on medical grounds

Employees, who are suspended from work on medical grounds (by virtue of a relevant provision in the **Ionising Radiations Regulations 1999**, the **Control of Lead at Work Regulations 2002**, or in a code of practice approved under s.16 of the **Health and Safety at Work, etc Act 1974**) are entitled (so long as they have been continuously employed for a period of not less than one month ending with the day before that on which the suspension begins) to be paid their normal remuneration while so suspended — unless their employer has offered them suitable alternative work to do (on terms and conditions no less favourable to them than those that applied to them in their regular work) and they have unreasonably refused to perform that work. (*Source:* ERA 1996, ss.64 and 65.) See also *suspension on maternity grounds*.

T

task-related contract

Means a contract of employment that, under its provisions determining how it will terminate in the normal course, is intended to terminate on the completion of a particular task (eg the installation and testing of a new software programme), or on the occurrence or non-occurrence of any other specific event (eg the return to work of an employee after maternity leave, or the cancellation of an expected order for goods or services). (*Source:* FTER 2002, regulation 1.) See also *fixed-term employee*.

141

tax credits

Under the **Tax Credits Act 2002**, which repealed and replaced the eponymous 2001 Act, employers throughout the UK are liable to pay Working Tax Credits to specified employees, when and as instructed to do so by the Tax Credits Office (TCO). The payments must be made through the payroll on normal paydays, with details recorded on the accompanying payslips. The relevant tax credits must be added to an employee's net pay, not to his or her gross pay. In other words, they are not liable to the deduction of tax or National Insurance Contributions (NICs) in their own right. The penalty for refusing or failing to pay tax credits through the payroll is a fine of up to £3000. Employees have the right not to be penalised, victimised or subjected to any other detriment (including dismissal) for being entitled to tax credits or for challenging their employer's failure to pay those credits.

termination of employment

See *dismissal, meaning of, notice of termination* and *wrongful dismissal*.

time off work: general

Employees nowadays have the legal right to a reasonable amount of paid or unpaid time off work to enable them to carry out their functions or duties as public officials, shop stewards, safety representatives, pension scheme trustees and the like. Redundant employees have the right to take time off to look for work; pregnant employees have the right to receive time off for antenatal care during normal working hours; and young persons aged 16 or 17 have the right to take time off to enable them to pursue studies or training leading to "relevant academic or vocational qualifications". Parents (and adopted parents) have the qualified right to take up to 13 weeks' unpaid parental leave; while others with dependants have the right to take time off at short notice to deal with a family emergency. Any employer, who unreasonably refuses to allow an employee to exercise his or her statutory right to time off will be answerable to an employment tribunal and could be ordered to pay such compensation as the tribunal considers to be just and equitable in the circumstances. In summary, the right to a reasonable period of time off is available to:

- trade union officials (shop stewards, etc) (paid)
- trade union members (unpaid)
- safety representatives (paid)
- pension scheme trustees (paid)
- employee representatives (paid)
- redundant employees (paid)
- young employees pursuing studies or training leading to a "relevant academic or vocational qualification" (paid)
- justices of the peace and members/officials of specified public bodies (unpaid)
- members of European Works Councils (EWCs) or "special negotiating bodies (SNBs)" (paid)
- pregnant employees needing ante-natal care (paid)
- parents of children under the age of five (or under the age of 18, if adopted) (unpaid) (See also *flexible working*)
- employees with responsibilities for dependants (unpaid)
- workers (whether employees or otherwise) accompanying other workers at disciplinary and grievance proceedings (paid).

An employer's unreasonable refusal to permit an employee to exercise his or her statutory right to time off work will inevitably lead to a complaint to an employment tribunal and an award of compensation. It is important to bear in mind that employees have no need to resign in order to pursue such complaints and will be awarded substantial amounts of compensation if they are disciplined, dismissed, selected for redundancy or subjected to any other detriment (eg a denial of an expected pay rise or overtime, or withholding opportunities for promotion, transfer or training) for presuming to question or challenge their employer's refusal or failure to accommodate those rights or for bringing proceedings before an employment tribunal or court. Save for redundant employees and people seeking to take parental leave, the rights listed above are available to all relevant employees regardless of their age or length of continuous service at the material time. (*Sources:* ERA 1996, **Pensions Act 1995**, TULRA 1992, **Collective Redundancies and Transfer of Undertakings (Protection of Employment) (Amendment) Regulations 1999; Transnational Information and Consultation of Employees Regulations 1999;** MPLR 1999 (as amended); **Right to Time Off for Study or Training Regulations 1999; Health and Safety (Consultation with Employees) Regulations 1996; Transfer of Undertakings (Protection of Employment) Regulations 1981; Safety Representatives and Safety Committees Regulations 1977.**) See also *antenatal care, dependants, time off for, look for work, time off to,* and *public duties, time off for.*

tips See *gratuities* and *national minimum wage.*

trade dispute Means a dispute between employers and workers, or between workers and workers, which is connected with one or more of the following matters:

- terms and conditions of employment, or the physical conditions in which any workers are required to work
- engagement or non-engagement, or termination or suspension of employment or the duties of employment, of one or more workers
- allocation of work or the duties of employment as between workers or groups of workers

- matters of discipline
- the membership or non-membership of a trade union on the part of a worker
- facilities for officials of trade unions
- machinery for negotiation or consultation, and other procedures, relating to any of the foregoing matters, including the recognition by employers or employers' associations of the right of a trade union to represent workers in any such negotiation or consultation or in the carrying out of such procedures. (*Source:* TULRA 1992, s.218.)

trade union　　Means an organisation that consists wholly or mainly of workers and whose principal purposes include the regulation of relations between workers and employers and employers' associations. Alternatively, it will consist wholly or mainly of constituent or affiliated organisations which fulfil the above conditions (or themselves consist wholly or mainly of constituent or affiliated organisations which fulfil those conditions); or representatives of such constituent of affiliated organisations, and whose principal purposes include the regulation of relations between workers and employers' associations, or the regulation of relations between its constituent or affiliated organisations. (*Source:* TULRA 1992, s.1.) See also *Certification Officer* and *independent trade union*

trade union dues　　See *"check-off" system (union dues)*.

trade union members (time off)　　Employees who are members of recognised independent trade unions have the right to be permitted a reasonable amount of unpaid time off work (at appropriate times and with their employer's prior agreement) to take part in any activities of that union (save for activities which themselves consist of industrial action, whether or not in contemplation or furtherance of a trade dispute). An employer's unreasonable refusal or failure to permit an employee to exercise his or her right to a period of unpaid time off for trade union activities (eg attendance at a meeting called by a shop steward to discuss the outcome of pay negotiations) will prompt such award of compensation as an employment tribunal considers to be just and equitable in the circumstances. (*Source:* TULRA 1992 s.170.) See also *time off work: general*.

trade union officials (time off)

Employees who are officials (shop stewards or works convenors) of an independent trade union, which is recognised by their employer as having collective bargaining rights for the entire workforce (or for one or more groups within the workforce) have the right to be permitted a reasonable amount of paid time off work to enable them to carry out such of their official duties as are concerned with pay and other terms and conditions of employment, working conditions, grievances and disciplinary matters affecting their members. They have the right also to be permitted a reasonable amount of time off on full pay to undergo training in those aspects of industrial relations that have a bearing on the matters in respect of which the union they represent have been granted negotiating rights, so long as the training in question has been approved by the Trades Union Congress (TUC) or by the employee's own union. An employer's refusal or failure to permit a trade union official to take a period (or periods) of time off for such purposes will prompt a complaint to an employment tribunal and such award of compensation as the tribunal considers to be just and equitable in the circumstances. (*Source:* TULRA 1992 s.168.) See also *time off work: general*.

trade union recognition

The granting of collective bargaining rights to an independent trade union in respect of a particular group (or groups) of employees within a particular employer's undertaking may be achieved either voluntarily or in consequence of a formal and valid request for recognition submitted to the relevant employer and submitted in accordance with the "trade union recognition" procedures laid down in Part I, Chapter VA and Schedule 1 to the **Trade Union and Labour Relations (Consolidation) Act 1992**. An employer may reject a request for trade union recognition if not wholly convinced that a majority of the workers in the bargaining unit in respect of which the union is seeking bargaining rights would be content to have the union negotiate terms and conditions of employment on their behalf. Nor need an employer respond if fewer than 10 per cent of the workers in the proposed bargaining unit are members of the trade union in question. An employer's rejection or failure to respond to any such request may be referred by the trade union in question to the Central Arbitration Committee (CAC) which will arbitrate and issue, where appropriate, a compulsory recognition order binding on both parties and enforceable by a court order. See also *Central Arbitration Committee, independent trade union* and *recognised independent trade union.*

trade union representatives

See *appropriate representatives*. See also *consultations: collective redundancies* and *consultations: transfers of undertakings.*

transfers of undertakings

Under the **Transfer of Undertakings (Protection of Employment) Regulations 1981**, an employer who purchases (or otherwise acquires, except through the purchase of shares) the whole or part of another employer's business or undertaking (as a going concern) also inherits the contracts of employment (and any and all associated liabilities and obligations under those contracts) of the persons employed in that business or undertaking (or part of that business or undertaking) immediately before the relevant transfer occurred. The subsequent dismissal of any of those employees — other than for an economic, technical or organisation reason unconnected with the transfer itself — is automatically unfair, as is any subsequent variation of the terms and conditions of employment enjoyed by the transferred employees when the sale or transfer took place. Employers contemplating the sale of their own business or undertaking (or a part of that undertaking) or the purchase of the whole or part of another business or undertaking are duty-bound to consult the appropriate representatives concerning their plans. This is a complex area of the law which has led to a great many (at times, seemingly contradictory) decisions by the tribunals and courts. The legislation demands further study and, if need be, professional advice. See also *consultations: transfers of undertakings*.

trust and confidence   See *fidelity and trust, duty of*.

TUPE   See *transfers of undertakings*.

U

unauthorised deductions from pay   See *deductions from pay*.

unfair dismissal, compensation for   See *additional award of compensation, basic award of compensation, compensatory award, dismissal, meaning ofinadmissible reasons for dismissal* and *supplementary award*.

union membership agreement   See *closed shop*.

unlawful reasons for dismissal   See *inadmissible reasons for dismissal*.

V

VDUs   See *display screen equipment.*

variation of contract   The unilateral variation of any provision in a contract of employment (or in any other contract) by one or other of the parties to that contract is a breach of contract entitling the other party to sue for damages. In the employment context, the unilateral imposition by an employer of a cut in pay or shorter working hours is a breach of contract entitling the employee to resign, with or without notice, and pursue a complaint of unfair constructive dismissal and/or a claim for damages before an employment tribunal. See also *gross misconduct, implied term* and *summary dismissal.*

vicarious liability   The common law principle which states that employers are liable for the acts of their employees if they are committed in the course of their employment. For example, employers are likely to be held liable for bullying or sexual harassment in the workplace if the evidence reveals that they had done little if anything to put an end to such conduct. "It is well-settled law that a master is liable, even for acts which he has not authorised, provided that they are so connected with the acts which he has authorised that they might rightly be regarded as modes, although improper modes, of doing them. On the other hand, if the unauthorised and wrongful act of the servant is not so connected with the authorised act as to be a mode of doing it but is an independent act, the master is not responsible, for in such a case the servant is not acting in the course of his employment but has gone outside it" (*Marsh v Moores* [1949] 2 All ER 27). The common law principle of vicarious liability has been imported into the **Sex Discrimination Act**

1975 (s.41(1)), the **Race Relations Act 1976** (s.31(1)), and the **Disability Discrimination Act 1995** (s.58(1)).

victimisation Employees and other workers, who are victimised, harassed, penalised or subjected to any other detriment — including termination of their contracts — by any act (or any deliberate failure to act) by their employers for exercising (or proposing to exercise) their statutory employment rights, or for challenging or questioning any alleged infringement of those rights (whether before an employment tribunal or otherwise) may complain to an employment tribunal and will be awarded substantial compensation if those complaints are upheld. Such complaints may be brought regardless of the age or length of service of the employees or workers in question. Nor need a would-be complainant resign in order to pursue such a complaint. (*Sources*: SDA 1975; RRA 1976; TULRA 1992; DDA 1995; ERA 1996; NMWA 1998; **Tax Credits Act 2002**; WTR 1998; PTWR 2000 and FTER 2002.

W

wage records, access to Workers who believe (on reasonable grounds) that they are not being paid the correct national minimum wage (NMW) have the right to require their employers to produce their wage records (in respect of one or more pay reference periods), to inspect and examine those records, and to copy any part of them. Workers may exercise that right alone or in the company of such other person as they think fit (such as an accountant or solicitor). To exercise that right, workers must serve a "production notice" on their employer requesting the production of the records in question. If the worker intends to be accompanied when those records are produced, the production notice must include a statement to that effect. The employer is duty-bound to comply within the next 14 days (or within such longer period as may be agreed). A failure to do so could prompt a complaint to an employment tribunal. Should that complaint be upheld, the employer will be ordered by the tribunal to pay a sum equal to 80 times the hourly amount of the NMW that should have been paid to the worker in question. To these ends, employers must maintain their payroll records for a period of three years beginning with the day upon which the pay reference period immediately following that to which they relate ends. (*Sources:* NMWA 1998, ss.11 and 12; NMWR 1999, regulation 38.)

wages, deductions from

See *deductions from pay*.

waiver clause

A clause in a fixed-term contact, or in a separate agreement attached to that contract, under which the employee in question agrees to waive his or her right to pursue a complaint of unfair dismissal (or to lay claim to a statutory redundancy payment) on the expiry and non-renewal of that contract. With the coming into force, on 25 October 1999, of the relevant provisions of the **Employment Relations Act 1999** and, on 1 October 2002, of related provisions in the **Fixed-term Employees (Prevention of Less Favourable Treatment) Regulations 2002**, and the concomitant repeal of s.197 of the **Employment Rights Act 1996**, dismissal and redundancy waiver clauses in fixed-term contracts are void and unenforceable. (*Sources:* ERA 1999, ss.8(1) and 44, and Schedule 9(3); FTER 2002, Schedule 2(3).)

week

For the purposes of determining an employee's period of continuous employment, a "week" is the period of seven consecutive days that ends on a Saturday. Otherwise, except in relation to the minimum period of notice required to terminate an employee's contract of employment, it means, in relation to an employee whose remuneration is calculated weekly by a week ending with a day other than a Saturday, a week ending with that other day, and, in relation to any other employee, a week ending with Saturday. (*Source:* ERA 1996, s.235.) See also *adoption pay period, maternity pay period* and *statutory paternity pay*.

week's pay

A week's pay, for the purposes of determining an employee's entitlement to a statutory redundancy payment, statutory maternity pay, statutory adoption pay, statutory paternity pay, statutory sick pay, a guarantee payment, payment on medical suspension, and the like, is the amount payable to that employee under the terms of his or her contract of employment. For an employee whose remuneration varies with the amount of work done, a week's pay is the average of the total remuneration paid to that employee over the period of 12 weeks (or, in some instances, eight weeks) immediately preceding the relevant calculation date. The relevant legislation is to be found in Part XIV, Chapter II of the **Employment Rights Act 1996**. An explanatory booklet, titled *Continuous employment and a week's pay: rules for calculation* (Ref: PL711) is available from the DTI Publications Orderline on 0870 1502 500 or from website www.dti.gov.uk.

week's pay, maximum amount of

The 2003/04 upper limit on the amount of a week's pay, for the purposes of calculating an employee's entitlement to a statutory redundancy payment is £260. That same upper limit applies to the calculation of the basic and additional awards of compensation for unfair dismissal (and the amount of any supplementary award); and the amount in respect of any one week payable to an employee in respect of any debt referable to a period time owed to an employee when his or her employer is insolvent. The upper limit on the amount of a week's pay for these purposes is reviewed and, where need be, rounded up or down to the nearest £10, in line with any rise or fall in the September on September Retail Prices Index (*Sources:* ERA 1996, s.227; ERA 1999, s.34; **Employment Rights (Increase of Limits) (No. 2) Order 2002**.) See also *insolvency of employers*.

weekly rest period   See *rest periods (daily and weekly)*.

"Whistle blower's" Act   See *Public Interest Disclosure Act 1998* and *protected disclosure*.

women, employment of   Legislation prohibiting or restricting the employment of women in certain occupations (notably in work involving exposure to lead or ionising radiations) is to be found in the **Ionising Radiations Regulations 1999**, and in the **Control of Lead at Work Regulations 2002**. Under the **Management of Health and Safety at Work Regulations 1999**, employers who employ women of child-bearing age must, when carrying out the risk assessment prescribed by those Regulations identify risks confronting new or expectant mothers (and/or their babies or developing foetuses) and take appropriate steps to eliminate or minimise those risks). If those risks are unavoidable, an employer must either transfer the employees in question to suitable alternative work or suspend them from work on full pay for so long as is necessary to avoid such risks. (*Source:* MHSAWR 1999, regulations 3 and 12.) See also *new or expectant mothers, risk assessment* and *suspension on maternity grounds*

work of equal value   See *equal value, work of*.

work permits   Any employer in the UK seeking to employ a foreign national subject to immigration control, who does not have the legal and subsisting right to live in, or take up employment while in, the UK, must apply to Work Permits (UK) (WP(UK)) — part of the Home Office's Immigration and Nationality Directorate — for a business and commerce work permit. Employers wishing to provide a non-EEC national with work experience or training leading to a recognised professional qualification must apply to WP(UK) for a Training and Work Experience Scheme (TWES) permit.

The prescribed form of application in either case is WP1 (or, for extensions to existing work permits, form WP1X). Copies of these forms (together with accompanying guidance notes and details of the Home Office's qualifying criteria for work permits) may either be downloaded from website www.workpermits-.gov.uk or obtained by telephoning WP(UK)'s distribution centre on 0990 210224. Work permit applications may be submitted to WP(UK) either electronically (by accessing the WP (UK) website www.workpermits.gov.uk, in which case, the relevant "smart" forms will appear automatically) or by post to:

Work Permits (UK)
Immigration and Nationality Directorate
Home Office
Level 5
Moorfoot
Sheffield S1 4PG

The following overseas workers do not need work permits:

(a) nationals of the European Economic Area (EEA) and citizens of Switzerland

(b) citizens of British Overseas Territories (BOTCs) (ie Anguilla, Bermuda, British

Antarctica, British Indian Ocean Territory, British Virgin Islands, Cayman Islands, Falkland Islands, Gibraltar, Monserrat, Pitcairn Islands, St Helena and Dependencies, South Georgia and the South Sandwich Islands, and the Turcs and Caicos Islands) — except those from Sovereign Base Areas in Cyprus

(c) Commonwealth citizens who are allowed to enter or remain in the UK on the basis that one or other of their grandparents was born in the UK

(d) the husbands, wives and dependent children under 18 of people who hold work permits or who qualify under any of the above categories, as long the endorsements in their passports place no restriction on their employment in the UK.

Please note that it is an offence under the **Asylum and Immigration Act 1996** to employ a foreign national aged 16 or over who is either an illegal immigrant or does not have the legal right to take up employment while in the UK. The penalty on summary conviction (for each offence) is a fine of up to £5000.

work rated as equivalent

Within the context of the **Equal Pay Act 1970**, a woman is to be regarded as employed on work rated as equivalent with that of any men if her job and their job have been given an equal value, in terms of the demand made on a worker under various headings (eg effort, skill or decision), in a study undertaken to evaluate in those terms the jobs to be done by the employees in an undertaking, or would have been given an equal value, but for the evaluation being made on a system setting different values for men and women on the same demand under any heading. (*Sources:* EqPA 1970, s.1(2)(b) and (5).)

155

worker

"Means an individual who has entered into or works under (or where the employment has ceased worked under):

(a) a contract of employment, or

(b) any other contract, whether express or implied and (if it is express) whether oral or in writing, whereby the individual undertakes to do, or perform personally, any work or services for another party to the contract whose status is not by virtue of the contract that of a client or customer of any profession or business undertaking carried on by the individual".

All workers (other than individuals who are genuinely self-employed) enjoy the protection afforded by legislation such as the **National Minimum Wage Act 1998**, the **Working Time Regulations 1998**, the **Part-time Workers (Prevention of Less Favourable Treatment) Regulations 2000**, and Part IVA of the **Employment Rights Act 1996** (Protected Disclosures). (*Sources:* ERA 1996, s.230(3); NMWA 1998, s.54(3); WTR 1998, regulation 2.) See also *agency worker*.

workforce agreement

An agreement is a "workforce agreement", for the purposes of the **Working Time Regulations 1998** and the **Maternity and Parental Leave, etc Regulations 1999** if:

(a) it is in writing

(b) it has effect for no more than five years

(c) it applies to all the relevant members of the workforce (or to all of the relevant members of the workforce who belong to a particular group)

(d) it is signed by elected representatives of the workforce (or in organisations with 20 or fewer workers, where no such representatives have been elected, by the majority of the workers in question); and

(e) before the agreement is made available for signature, the employer provided all the affected workers with copies of the text of the agreement and any such guidance notes as those workers might reasonably require in order to understand it fully. (*Sources:* WTR 1998, regulations 5, 6(1), 11(4), 12(2), 13(3), 14(3) and 15(5); MPLR 1999, regulation 16(1).)

working hours

See *hours of work: workers aged 18 and over* and *hours of work: workers under the age of 18.*

Working Time Regulations 1998

Under the 1998 Regulations, which came into force on 1 October 1998, every worker has the legal right to a minimum four weeks' paid annual holidays, in-work rest breaks, and daily and weekly rest periods. Adult workers also have the right not to be required to work for more than an average of 48 hours a week or for more than an average eight hours at night in any 24-hour period. Workers under the age of 18 may not be required to work for more than eight hours a day or for more than 40 hours in any week; for the most part they may not be employed at night during the restricted period. There is no provision for the averaging of a young worker's working hours; nor may a young worker opt-out of those restrictions. The 1998 Regulations do not apply to "special case" workers (eg dock workers, postal workers, hospital workers); workers employed in excluded sectors (notably transport workers); domestic workers, or workers covered by collective or workforce agreements modifying the application of some (but by no means all) of a worker's rights under those Regulations. (*Source:* WTR 1998, as amended, in the case of young workers by the **Working Time (Amendment) Regulations 2003**.) A comprehensive guide to the 1998 Regulations is available from the DTI's Publications Orderline on 0870 1502 500. See also *annual holidays, health assessment, health and capabilities assessment, hours of work: workers aged 18 and over, hours of work: workers under the age of 18, rest breaks, rest periods (daily and weekly),* and *young worker.*

written statement of employment particulars

Every employee has the legal right to be provided with a written statement outlining the principal terms and conditions of his or her employment. The statement (often, if incorrectly, referred to as the "contract of employment") must be issued within two months of the date on which the employee first started work; or, if the employee is to be sent abroad for one month or more, before the employee leaves the UK. Any term in the written statement which purports to undermine (or override) an employee's statutory employment rights is null and void. An employer may withhold the statement from an employee who resigns or is dismissed within one month of starting work, but not otherwise — even if an employee quits or is sacked within the two-month deadline for issuing the statement.

The following particulars must be included in the written statement. If there are no particulars to be entered under any of heads (a) to (o) below (eg if an absentee employee is not entitled to sick pay, other than statutory sick pay (SSP)), that fact must be stated. A "Nil" return is not acceptable. An employer may choose to issue the written statement either as a single document containing all of the particulars required by items (a) to (o) below or issue it in instalments — so long as one of those instalments (the "principal statement") includes the particulars required by items (a) to (h) inclusive.

The particulars in question are:

(a) the names of the employer and the employee

(b) the date when the employment began

(c) the date on which the employee's period of continuous employment began (taking into account any employment with a previous employer which counts towards that period)

(d) the employee's job title (or a brief description of the work that he or she has been employed to do)

(e) the employee's place of work or, if required or permitted to work at various places, a statement to that effect, and the employer's address

(f) the employee's scale or rate of pay or the method to be used to calculate pay (as well as rates or allowances payable in respect of overtime and shift working, bonus and commission payments; and so on)

(g) the intervals at which wage or salary payments are to be made (eg weekly or monthly) and the method of payment (cash, cheque or credit transfer)

(h) the employee's working hours, including the pattern of working hours (eg Monday to Friday, inclusive), daily starting and finishing times, and intervals for meals and rest (paid or unpaid)

(i) if the employment is not intended to be permanent, or is for a fixed term, the period for which it is expected to continue, or the date on which it is to end

(j) the employee's entitlement to holidays, including public and bank holidays (the particulars given being sufficient to enable the employee to calculate his or her entitlement to accrued holiday pay on the termination of his or her employment

(k) the employee's qualified right (if any), other than any entitlement to SSP, to be paid his or her normal wages or salary (or a proportion of them) if absent from work because of illness or injury

(l) any terms and conditions relating to pensions and pension schemes, plus confirmation of the existence or otherwise of a contracting-out certificate issued in accordance with Chapter 1 of Part III of the **Pensions Schemes Act 1993** (stating that the employee's employment is contracted-out employment for the purposes of the **1993 Act**)

(m) the length of notice which the employee is required to give, and entitled to receive, to terminate his or her employment

(n) any collective agreement which directly affects the employee's terms and conditions of employment (including, where the employer is not a signatory to that agreement, the names of the parties or organisations party to that agreement)

(o) if the employee is required to work outside the UK for one month or more, an indication of the likely length of that overseas assignment, the currency in which the employee is to be paid while overseas, any additional remuneration or benefits to be paid or provided during the employee's absence, and any terms and conditions relative to the employee's return to the UK.

Given the inevitable complexity of an employer's occupational sick pay and pension schemes, the particulars to be given in items (k) and (l) may refer the employee to the existence and ready accessibility of one or more other documents which explain those matters in greater detail. If the employer does not operate an occupational sick pay or pension scheme, the employee must be made aware of that fact in the written statement itself.

In a business or organisation employing 20 or more persons (including people employed at another branch of the employer's business, or by an associated employer), the written statement must also include a note specifying any disciplinary rules applicable to the employee (or referring the employee to some other document, such as a staff or works handbook, which explains those rules — so long as that other document is readily accessible to the employee). The note or other document must also explain the likely consequences, and the procedures to be followed if those rules are broken, and give the name or job title of the person (such as a supervisor or manager) to whom the employee can appeal if dissatisfied with any disciplinary decision taken against him or her. The note must also explain the employer's procedures for dealing with and resolving employee grievances. For further details, see *disciplinary and dismissal procedures* and *grievances and procedure*.

Any change in the particulars included in the written statement must be notified in writing to each affected employee at the earliest opportunity, but not later than one month after the change in question. A failure to provide the written statement may lead to a reference to an employment tribunal. Once the relevant provisions of the **Employment Act 2002** come into force, an employer's failure to provide an employee with a written statement will lead to an increase in the amount of compensation otherwise payable to that employee by the equivalent of between two and four weeks' pay. (*Sources:* ERA 1996, ss.1-7; EA 2002, ss.35-38.)

written statement of reasons for dismissal An employee who has been dismissed, with or without notice, for a reason other than pregnancy or childbirth (see below), and who had been continuously employed for one year or more at the *effective date of termination* of his or her contract of employment, may apply to his or her employer for a written statement explaining the reasons for dismissal. An employer who fails to respond to such a request within the next 14 days will be ordered by an employment tribunal to pay the employee a sum equal to the amount of two weeks' pay. (*Source:* ERA 1996, ss.92 and 93.)

An employer who dismisses a pregnant employee (for whatever reason) or dismisses an employee after childbirth (during her ordinary or additional maternity leave period) must provide that employee with a written statement explaining the reasons for her dismissal, whether or not she has asked for any such statement and regardless of her length of continuous service at the material time (ERA, ss.92(4) and 93).

wrongful dismissal   An employee is treated in law as having been wrongfully dismissed by his or her employer if the employee is dismissed without benefit of reasonable notice (or the notice laid down in the employee's contract, or the statutory minimum period of notice prescribed by s.86 of the **Employment Rights Act 1996**) in circumstances which did not (or did not appear to) justify summary or instant dismissal. A claim for damages arising out of a wrongful dismissal may be presented to an employment tribunal or county court. However, the upper limit on the amount of damages that may be awarded by the employment tribunals for wrongful dismissal is £25,000. (*Sources:* **Employment Tribunals Extension of Jurisdiction (England and Wales) Order 1994; Employment Tribunals Extension of Jurisdiction (Scotland) Order 1994.**)

XYZ

young person

A young person is a person under the age of 18. Legislation prohibiting or restricting the employment of young persons is to be found in the **Ionising Radiations Regulations 1999** and in the **Control of Lead at Work Regulations 2002**. Furthermore, when conducting the risk assessment exercise prescribed by regulation 3 of the **Management of Health and Safety at Work Regulations 1999**, every employer who employs people under the age of 18 (including school age children) must take particular account of the risks confronting young persons. It should take into account their relative immaturity and inexperience; their (at times) cavalier attitude to workplace risks; the nature, degree and extent of their exposure to potentially harmful physical, biological and chemical agents; and the amount of health and safety training (if any) that each of them has received.

The Regulations further caution that young persons may not be employed in work that is beyond their physical or psychological capabilities; work that involves harmful exposure to toxic or carcinogenic substances or agents; work involving the risk of accidents that young persons cannot reasonably foresee or recognise; or work in which there is a risk to health from cold, heat, noise or vibration — unless the work is necessary for training purposes (under the supervision of competent persons) and reasonable steps have been taken to minimise those risks. See also *children, employment of, hours of work: workers under the age of 18* and *risk assessment*.

young workers

Workers under the age of 18 may not lawfully be employed for more than eight hours a day, or for more than 40 hours in any week. Nor (with few exceptions) may they be employed at night

163

during the "restricted period" (ie between the hours of 10.00pm and 6.00am or, if their contracts require them to work after 10.00pm, between the hours of 11.00pm and 7.00am). These upper limits and restrictions are absolute. There is no provision for the averaging of a young worker's working hours over a reference period; nor (unlike adult workers) may young workers opt-out of those limits. (*Source:* **Working Time Regulations 1998**, as amended by the **Working Time (Amendment) Regulations 2002**.) See also *hours of work: workers under the age of 18.*

zero hours contracts A person employed under a so called "zero hours contract" has no entitlement to a regular weekly income and is paid only for the time he or she actually works. However, such a contractual arrangement (although giving the employer a degree of flexibility) is likely to fall foul of the **Working Time Regulations 1998**, not to mention the **National Minimum Wage Regulations 1999**, if the employee in question is required to remain "on standby" in the employer's premises (against the possibility of work being available). That same rule applies to workers working at home who, for example, are obliged to be available throughout the night to deal with occasional telephone calls diverted to their homes from their employer's central switchboard — even if no such calls are received or they occupy their time between calls sleeping, watching TV or undertaking domestic chores (as decided by the Court of Appeal in *British Nursing Association v Inland Revenue (National Minimum Wage Compliance Team)* [2002] IRLR 480). There was a similar decision in *Wright v Scottbridge Construction Ltd* [2001] IRLR 589. In that case, it was held that a night-watchman in a factory (whose primary duty was to respond to a fire or intruder alarm) was entitled to be paid the national minimum wage for each of the 14 hours of his shift, even though he spent the majority of those 14 hours asleep on a bed provided for him by his employer.